Dreams, Nightmares and Pursuing the Passion

Personal Perspectives on
College and University
Leadership

by Shannon Ellis

Dreams, Nightmares and Pursuing the Passion: Personal Perspectives on College and University Leadership.

Additional copies may be purchased by contacting the NASPA publications department at 301-638-1749.

ISBN: 0-931654-31-9

By Shannon Ellis, Ph.D.
Vice President for Student Services, University of Nevada, Reno

Contents

Introduction

This book is about being a Vice President for Student Services – a new one, taking on this role for the first time in my career.

It was written at the suggestion of Dr. Gwendolyn Jordan Dungy, Executive Director of the National Association of Student Personnel Administrators (NASPA). In July 1998, two weeks before I began my first vice presidency, she gave me two blank journals and asked me to write about anything and everything over the course of the next year.

That I did – at bedtime, early in the morning, before a run, on airplanes, in restaurants, during legislative hearings and board meetings, Sunday afternoons in front of a fireplace, sitting in my car, and waiting for the doctor, veterinarian, and dentist. At various times I was mad, confused, elated, exhausted, triumphant, or enamored, but I was always thrilled to finally be a Vice President for Student Services, proud to be a member of NASPA, and very fortunate to have a best friend in Gwen Dungy.

Talk about a woman with vision and foresight. There is no way I would have remembered these stories, lessons, feelings, anxieties, and people if Gwen had not given me the blank journals. Thanks for asking, Gwen. Thanks also to my "editor," a retired journalist and 7th grade English teacher, who also happens to be my mother. She spent many hours with red pen in hand, helping me create a concise and coherent piece. Magnificent Publications, Inc. took my long string of thoughts and made them sound great. Thank you.

The author and columnist Pete Hamill said writers "should only write the book they were meant to write and no more." I am not a writer by profession. I am a student affairs professional by good fortune, great advice, harsh feedback, keen failures, kind mentors, and startling revelations. Thank you to all before me who opened their arms wide and welcomed me into their world. They were men such as Willard

2

Broom, Bill Field, Jeremy Stringer, Jim Appleton, and Jim Dennis. They were women such as Gail Martin, Marjorie Peace Lenn, and Marie Kotter. Each made me believe I was able to achieve and provided me with opportunities to excel.

I began my first vice presidency on Monday, August 10, 1998, three days after the bombing of the U.S. Embassy in Kenya. I felt more keenly than ever the importance of educating students for leadership, and I started work determined to lead through inspiration and innovation. In a world beset with violence, it seemed essential to me that we create an environment truly dedicated to helping students learn. It remains so for me to this day.

1. Moving Up

The Dream

September 29, 1998. I wake up in the middle of the night. It takes me a while to remember where I am. Nevada? How did I get here?

My chance to become a Vice President for Student Services came somewhere between Phoenix and Seattle, just after New Year's Day 1998, as my husband and I drove home from visiting my parents for the holidays. At one point in the long trip I asked my husband, who had retired young, if he thought he would ever go back to work. Rich had been a brilliant lawyer on a fast track when the company he worked for, and in which he owned a considerable amount of stock, was sold. I thought he'd enjoy the break this unexpected wealth brought him but would soon thirst for the competitive fun and challenging stress of corporate law.

"Go back to work? Why would I want to do that?" he said. My answer was not to his question but, rather, to my *real* agenda: "Then I'd like to become a Vice President for Student Affairs."

He understood this was the pinnacle of my career and strongly supported the idea, and the negotiations began at once. Not for a job, mind you, but between the two of us. We established some criteria that would make us both happy and arrived at parameters for my job search that were somewhat limiting but provided enough clear guidance. I would try to find a job in the West near the water, preferably the ocean, and we would move East only if it was on the coast.

Not three weeks later, I got an email from Pru Jones at the University of Nevada-Reno, encouraging me to apply for the VP opening there. Pru had served as a member of NASPA's Region 5 Advisory Board when I was regional Vice President. I emailed her back, "Thanks for thinking of me, but I don't think so." There was no ocean, and, to be honest, I couldn't picture Nevada as a place to advance my career.

But over the next few weeks, when I was out on a long run or puttering about the garden, my thoughts returned to Reno. I told my husband I was going to apply for the Vice President's job, "just to get my feet wet."

"Tell Me What You Want"

August 1, 1998. Sometimes I wonder, just how did I get this great job?

The interview process – first by phone and then in person – was very positive. It had been eight years since I'd been on the market, and I looked at the whole experience as an excellent opportunity to sharpen my interview skills and gain a sense of what was required. It went well and I was asked back for a second interview.

My husband joined me on the trip, and we had dinner with the former Vice President. "You know," she said, "I'm supposed to talk you into taking this job." I knew her from NASPA activities and felt comfortable asking her sensitive questions. She gave me pointers about salary negotiations, other Vice Presidential players, working with the President, and many other useful insights. Everyone should be so fortunate as to have such an ally.

When I met with the President the next day, he made it clear that they wanted me. I made it clear I was interested and asked a number of questions, which he answered thoroughly but he made no salary offer. I did not want to offer up the first number. We danced around the issue: he asked me what I required, I said it depended on what the other Vice Presidents and my predecessor made, he reminded me that they had all been there quite some time. Much to my amazement we ended the meeting without a specific salary being mentioned.

What arrived in the mail a few days later was a very decent offer. I knew it was decent because in front of me I had figures for the salary of every Vice President, their years of experience, size of their budgets, number of staff in their divisions, and scope of responsibilities. I had culled this information from public documents, from the Vice Presidents themselves, and from annual salary surveys conducted by

NASPA and NACUBO. As negotiations with the President progressed, he finally said, "Just tell me what you want." I did. And he agreed.

The Art of Changing Jobs

August 5, 1998. I have a sense, hard to define, that a member of my staff is considering another job.

My father often said to me, "How you leave a job is as important as how you start one." I had immediately told my supervisor at The Evergreen State College that I would be searching for a Vice President's position in the next year, but made it clear that I was not resigning. He was very supportive, as always, but clearly surprised when I told him a month later I had been invited for a campus interview.

Telling the terrific secretary in my office was the hardest, even though the Nevada job was by no means a sure thing. She had left a good job elsewhere in the college the year before and was an amazing contributor to our work in the Dean's office. She and her sister were about to take a well-deserved trip East and I didn't want her to worry about her job security. She took the news well and was assured that her position was not in jeopardy.

A few days later, I was met at the Reno-Tahoe airport by the search committee chair. As we walked to the parking structure, the secretary from my Evergreen office approached from the opposite direction. I was stunned! Her sister had surprised her with a trip to Las Vegas and their plane had been diverted to Reno due to mechanical problems. I introduced her to the committee chair and we all parted ways, laughing. What if I had not told her of my interview plans? Careful honesty is a good policy.

2. Being a Vice President

Business as Usual

August 10, 1998. First day. Everyone is incredibly nice to me. Wonder how long this will last.

What is your worst nightmare about the first day in a new job?

- $25,000 in cash is taken from the safe.
- Your new boss, the President, won't be back for a week.
- You need to find $350,000 for an overrun on a building project.

- A victim of sexual assault advises you of her lawsuit against you and the university.
- Your new dining facility HVAC system is blocking the view of the English faculty.
- A student asks you for directions.

How about all of the above? I knew that this was business as usual in student affairs, but in a new job it can seem overwhelming. You don't know the people, the policies, the procedures, or the politics that make such days routine.

When I asked Vice Presidential colleagues about their first day I heard other terrifying stories. One got a call at 2 a.m.: a campus police officer had been axed to death on campus. Another learned that the lead financial officer in the division was being charged with embezzlement. One colleague learned that the Academic Affairs Vice President had died. Much to the resentment of faculty, my colleague was asked to assume his duties. A handful discovered that their presidents were leaving or, in one case, had left. It can be equally terrifying when an administrative assistant leaves, since this is someone who can make or break you in that first week, month, year, or at any time.

So by anybody's standards, my first day was calm. I left before 6 p.m. and went out to dinner with my husband, thinking, "This Vice President thing is a piece of cake!"

What Remains, What Changes

September 5, 1998. We make it to Labor Day weekend! A recap of the first four weeks of work and first two weeks of school: dealt with two suicides and wrote two letters of condolence, convened and charged five committees, scheduled 133 appointments, gave 21 speeches, and made changes all over in quiet little ways.

It never occurred to me that I would write about workload in a book about being a new Vice President for Student Services. After all, in prior positions at other schools I had dealt with the bizarre, the litigious, and the stressful. I've had two staff say they did not get along because a psychic told them they were scorned lovers in a former life. Plenty of people have threatened to sue, and some have acted on their threats. Students and staff have died – some slowly and many suddenly, some by their own hands or at the hands of others. I've cut many more budgets than I've increased and withstood the wrath of crazed supervisors, parents, alumni, students, and public officials.

But the pace this first month was intense. I had a lot of homework before each meeting. I wanted to be polished and calm and *never* late. In short, I wrote, "You want to seem perfect." Why? People are unforgiving, and I believed I needed to strive to be worthy of their respect and their hard work each day. As a leader, as *the* leader, I felt I owed that to the staff. I still do.

The internal and external demands were and are immense. I love both and constantly ready myself to "switch hats" with comfort and ease. In a single morning, meetings can move from the personal to the administrative, from inspiring leadership to political maneuvering. Each demands a different mindset, a specific set of skills and language, even a specialized personal demeanor.

Nothing Personal

September 27, 1998. Sunday morning. Worked much of yesterday and will go back at it again today. Making headway.

Maintaining perspective has become more important as I have matured professionally. At one time, a typo in the commencement program could send me to my office on the verge of tears. A professional disagreement with a colleague made it impossible to be her friend. Now, I realize that disagreements in the workplace can just as easily lead to an energetic and innovative climate as to one of division and dissension. It is really true when we say to ourselves and one another, "Don't take it personally."

Wrestling the Gorilla

October 11, 1998. All of us with PhDs know that we are no smarter than a lot of people who don't have them. What we do know is that we stuck it out, inside and outside the classroom, for all the years it took.

When an interviewer asked astronaut Buzz Aldrin what he would do with his last few minutes of life if he were in a space capsule and everything had gone wrong, he replied, "I'd spend every last minute working like crazy to fix it."

Persistence. I once heard a commencement speaker talk about the importance of this trait, saying, "When wrestling a gorilla, you don't quit when you get tired. You quit when the gorilla gets tired." I like to think that, in the day of a Student Affairs Vice President, every gorilla I encounter gets tired before I do.

In fact, I often imagine the problem as a gorilla. People sitting across the table from me with issues needing to be resolved take on the qualities of a gorilla. Memos requesting a 5% budget cut by next week grow four legs and lumber through tropical forests. Letters of complaint about Student Services in the student newspaper glare and snort. Another Vice President charging into my turf is merely beating his chest and baring his teeth. This is my favorite image; I have found myself needing to stifle a smile at the conference table.

Building Trust – Part One

October 23, 1998. There is no doubt in my mind that we work in an institution – higher education – that is misunderstood by the public, held to increasing standards of accountability, and viewed as an entitlement for which little should be paid out of pocket.

Even worse, many students and parents seem to want what the 1993 Wingspread Group called a "credential without content." Despite all that, Americans and people around the world still have respect for higher education in this country. It is ours to lose.

So, as an SSAO, what will you do to rebuild the trust with legislators, parents, neighbors, and prospective students in kindergarten today?

An important first step may be public reaffirmation of the value and role of learning. As Academics and Student Services alike place student learning at the center of the academy, we can begin to educate and enlighten our important public. I've stumped this to neighborhood groups, Rotary clubs, city councils, the state assembly, NAACP, Latin Chamber of Commerce, and K-12 Educational Collaborative. I'll debate and discuss it with anyone who will listen.

This cannot be accomplished through one-way edicts shared during recruitment and public hearings. It can be moved forward through honest and civil debate that should evolve into partnerships for reform and renewal.

Let Problems Be Problems

November 5, 1998. You know the old proverb, "Problems are disguised opportunities." Let's be honest, problems can be a big pain.

Problems can consume positive energy and time needed for more visionary tasks and progressive accomplishments.

A ground rule: Avoid the problem in the first place.

You and your staff need to train yourselves always to ask, "What are the potential problems with this issue?" Especially when you are new, taking the time to think about potential problems, discuss them with others, and come up with solutions in advance will save time, energy, and even money.

Lawyers have been trained to "take the other side" as they prepare their best case. Student Affairs would be wise to do the same. This means, of course, we must be open to people and perspectives in opposition to our ideals and goals. Listening may be hard, but cultivating the ability to "listen deeply" will serve us well. Go to the opposition's turf prepared to hear its side, ask questions in order to gain a greater understanding and, if appropriate, answer questions.

Leader as Administrator

Leader or administrator? On any given day, one role will overshadow the other. Overall, a new Vice President needs to have many excellent days as both.

Being inspiring and innovative, visionary and supportive, is never enough. Administrative tasks loom large and broad for SSAOs. I think of them as providing structure, process, and, most important, context for whatever needs to be managed – budget, reorganization, a new program, or a new hire. Mastering administration sets your effectiveness for years to come, and you'll bank on these strengths when you have the occasional weak moment.

Sound a bit impersonal? Perhaps being a manager is exactly that, but it still involves combining people and ideas to establish strategies and make decisions.

Our Role as Convener

November 11, 1998. Veterans Day: A day off! Rich is in Chicago for a legal seminar and I bring home piles of paper to work on. At least a change of venue from the office will give me a bit of a break. I have settled into a pattern of very little sleep, a lot of human interaction at a fairly deep but quick level, and many unfinished talks.

Student Affairs Vice Presidents need to excel at getting people to come together around the table to discuss the "three Ps and one S" – policies, procedures, problems, and solutions.

At least three times a day a colleague, staff member, or student leader talks about an issue important to them but with no sense of the next steps to address and resolve it. On my better days I ask "What does so-and-so say when you talk to him about this?" And the frequent response? "Oh, I haven't talked to him."

Well, that's not going to get the item resolved. When staff show deep reluctance to talk to the key person involved, I ask, "If this were an issue in your area and she came to me about it, wouldn't you want me to tell her to talk to you directly?" Usually the answer is yes. It is then good to ask, "Who else should be involved in the conversation?"

Student Services seems to have experience and abilities to be a good convener. We try to stay nimble by pulling together seemingly opposing or unrelated people and groups into action teams, problem solvers, and strategic alliances. Use your intelligence to end the divisiveness and hopelessness that characterize our campuses. Discontinue the idea of superiority or inferiority that has plagued our profession.

The convener role does not always emerge from a god-like self-perception or an attempt to fill a leadership vacuum. It has become increasingly clear that our campus issues cannot be solved within separate silos characterized by rigid traditions. A modern college of any type, size, and location is so complicated that issues must be addressed by the whole, in the whole.

Most significant in my first year was bringing academic leaders and student senators together for more diversity in the core curriculum. A perceived need for more diversity in the curriculum cannot be understood in isolation, it is part of a larger issue. And I think our role as conveners is especially vital when the item involves student experience that does not fall under our formal organizational duties.

Many people react with fear, confusion, and even anger. I have learned the value of picking up the phone and having conversations about the issue before telling them I am gathering a small group to talk things out. I never ask permission to do so. Sometimes one meeting does it; often it is a time of breaking the ice and struggling to find mutual areas of agreement so we can build trust and make progress.

Why Would It Have Crossed My Mind?

November 14, 1998. A day of alumni brunches, a football game, visits to tailgaters. Last night was the International Affairs Club annual cultural dinner and performances, as well as a speech at the fraternity installation dinner (luckily, in the same building). This hectic schedule is not letting up. I can't even schedule "fake" appointments to get caught up and prepare for the next meeting. My own projects, such as personnel issues, budget concerns, policy compliance and revision, and other vice presidential responsibilities, are getting lost.

It should have crossed my mind, but it didn't, that in addition to fulfilling a schedule like this I was expected to donate money to the school where I worked. For most of my career, I was paid at the lower end of the scale. No one seemed to expect that I would contribute, not even at the University of Southern California – the fundraising Mecca. The institution obviously knew my salary and the cost of living in southern California and put me on the "do not solicit" list.

Imagine my surprise when I attended NASPA's first Alice Manicur Symposium for Women Aspiring to be Senior Student Affairs Officers in Boston. A panel of women Vice Presidents told us we were expected to give a "significant" portion of our salaries to the institution. They cited donations ranging from $1,000 to $10,000. I remember we all turned to one another, dumbfounded, and laughed about giving not only 24 hours, seven days a week, blood, sweat, and tears, but now *money.*

My first thought was to be grateful. It was worth the trip to Boston to learn this now and not later. It made sense. If we are asking individuals, government, and foundations to give, it makes sense for senior leadership to put our money where our mouths are.

On my second interview at Nevada my husband and I had dinner with the former Vice President, who said that she donated $3,000 and spread it around to various groups on campus. When I negotiated my salary I made sure to get that extra $3,000 to cover the expectation.

After I started my job I made the rounds and met with each of my fellow Vice Presidents in their offices. I asked the Vice President for Development about the expectation of a Vice President. Much to my surprise, he said $1,000. I had mixed feelings; my predecessor had obviously done better than I did in the salary department, but my out-of-pocket expenses looked more manageable now. At first, I went with the $1,000. Over the years I have added gifts for good causes such as women's athletics, a transition fund for international students getting settled in America, and emergency loans for students in need.

Small Town Talk, Big Misunderstandings

December 19, 1998. A snowstorm brings 4 inches today. Even though finals and midyear commencement are over, we are busy! I am unraveling some issues arising from poor communication...or no communication.

In my first year, the Intramurals and Recreation Program let me know, via an intermediary, that they wanted out of their academic home and into Student Services. Would I take them? Their rationale was strong and my research revealed many good reasons for the change. Since student fees funded most of the program, the Student Senate came forward with an initiative to make the move.

The fact that it made sense was not the problem. I was in no way interested in doing a "department grab," especially during my first year. Campuses are small towns and I knew word would get out. I went straight to the Academic Dean. "People are talking," I told her, and I related what I was hearing. She told me all the reasons that transferring Intramurals and Recreation to our Division was a bad idea. I learned a lot. I passed word along via the intermediary that I would accept their program, but only if it was given to me. The idea never came up again.

Name That Tune Your Own

December 21, 1998. Hey! I made it through my first semester as VP. It went fast, but we made headway. Created a climate where we can improve conditions and not just have people sit and gripe. Last Wednesday's year-end breakfast for all staff was a huge success. Over 100 attended and were of good cheer. Two assessment workshops are scheduled for February.

As I passed the one-semester landmark, I stumbled onto an idea that made great sense to me: Find your song. I was rather late getting into the Ally McBeal club, but reruns at odd hours captivated me. Her therapist asks her to select a theme song that symbolizes her aspirations, dreams, and abilities, and to sing it every time she needs to boost her confidence. Ally McBeal chose the fast-paced "I Know Something About Love."

Then I read a quote from Goddard College's Barbara Mossberg, who said she was probably the only University President to have "Cockeyed Optimist" from Rogers and Hammerstein's *South Pacific* played at her inauguration.

"Hmm…," I wrote in my journal, "There must be something to this."

What will be your theme song? You don't have to have it played at your inauguration. You don't have to reveal it to anyone. You can keep it completely to yourself – in fact, that probably is a good idea. It gives you strength and power, a secret weapon in the thousands of touchy situations experienced by a Vice President, especially a new one.

You can sometimes make light of the normal politics and shenanigans of higher education, but there are also times when dead serious is what you must be. You must maintain calm, serve as a role model for the behavior you seek from others, and stay focused on priority tasks.

And my theme song? On this I am going to follow my own advice and stay mum.

Building Trust – Part Two

January 12, 1999. Despite our differences, I am confident we can find common ground. Sometimes a shared enemy forges strange alliances. A crisis will establish a sudden coalition. Simply being asked and listened to can go a long way.

I recall clearly a two-hour meeting in which residents in the University's neighborhood were invited to hear about master planning on campus. We sat around a large table, and after my five-minute opening, the barrage of complaints began: noisy students, vandalism, threats to property and person, and traffic.

Two neighbors told me the University should move – after 120 years, longer than their homes had been there. Another told me the faculty and staff could stay, but students and classes should move to the south of town where there was plenty of property. All of these folks had been long-time employees of the University and were now retired.

I nodded, replied when I could, rectified misinformation, and made no excuses. Mostly, I listened and let the residents vent. Then, I went back to the University and began following up on any problems we could address. The next time we met with residents, we sensed greater trust. Things continued to improve. Of course, some were never satisfied. We put up stop signs in key points on a side road, to slow down the traffic past homes where neighbors had complained. I asked one homeowner how he liked the signs. He said he hated them – they made the traffic too slow!

Be Prepared To Grieve

February 20, 1999. I return from a funeral and a fairly senior staff member asks where I was. I tell him, and he says he could never have done that: "I don't do funerals." I tell him I understand. But I hope he never becomes a Vice President.

Acquaintance or stranger, suicide or accident, murder or terminal illness, graduate or undergraduate student – as SSAO I attend all their funerals.

Prior to becoming Vice President, I attended only if it was someone I knew. Those were hard enough, but I feel that a caring, learning community extends to all our students. This is especially true when the turnout is sparse. Then, I sit with parents, siblings, roommates, and significant others, talking, looking at pictures, listening. Other memorials are jam-packed and simply introducing myself as from the University and signing the guest book may be all I do. Buddhist, African American, Catholic, rural, gang member, mother of two, father of three, cheerleader, cellist, and genius – their ceremonies remain in my head and are written in my journal.

It is not uncommon that I am asked to give a eulogy, even for students I do not know. I always say yes.

There Is Something About March

March 4, 1999. I am struggling to paint the big picture for students and Student Services and also deal with the day-to-day. I seem to spend more and more time on cleanup.

March definitely came in like a lion. Even good leaders and managers – even *great* ones – become overwhelmed. One of the smartest things we do in our Division is to keep meticulous notes and files. It's a habit I developed in my first Student Affairs job as Director of Greek Affairs, and it comes from a lifetime of hearing "What's the worst that can happen?"

We have often avoided the worst-case scenario through our ability to reconstruct action and conversations in a quick turnaround. Notes alone won't do it. Not a week goes by that I don't discuss with senior staff the scenario of "when you are on the stand in a court of law and the opposing lawyer asks what you did to educate students and avoid this tragedy, how well could you answer the question?"

Paradoxical Traits of a Leader

March 6, 1999. In Reinventing Leadership, *Bennis and Townsend ask, "What are some of the paradoxical traits a leader might possess?" One of their answers: "patience and urgency." Good. I'm not crazy after all.*

While I am patient with people to get a job done, I also light little fires to move things up on the priority list. It is a very sensitive balance.

Bennis and Townsend mention another paradox I have written about: A leader must be visible and available but not to the extent that dependency or panic results when the leader is not around. To make myself available, I began to get my house in order – working some late nights and weekends, delegating authority, catching up on paperwork and phone calls – so that I could focus on crafting my vision and setting my course.

I often arrange to meet with staff, faculty, or students in their own "quarters" so I can get out to new places around campus. Otherwise, I may enter my building in the morning and not leave it again until I go home. I also try to schedule time to wander around campus and make an appearance at career fairs, cultural festivals, faculty receptions, and awards ceremonies. I enjoy the celebrations and traditions, and my visit often means a great deal to the organizers and participants.

Brevity, Soul, Wit

March 19, 1999. If I give one more speech, I'll scream. I used to like speaking in public. I know it is my way to platform ideas and expectations so that the culture will change. I know it can inspire people at times when they most need it. But who will inspire me?

Speeches. You give a lot of them. In my first 10 days on the job I gave 14 speeches to student groups, families, community members, staff, faculty, high school counselors, principals, new students, nontraditional students, city council members – you name them and I'll bet I gave them a speech.

While I came to focus on similar themes, I had to work hard to avoid giving the same speech, since audiences often overlapped. I repeated certain messages deliberately to raise strategic issues and send up trial balloons. Not long after I began to attend events in my official capacity, I would be asked to say a few words with no prior notice. I quickly learned to have brief comments in my head, on a napkin, or once on the palm of my hand.

Brief is good. Making three or five points in a succinct manner is a reliable way to keep things straight and help your audience retain the message. But the best strategy is telling a great story, as long as it has relevance to the occasion.

It Never Ends

March 22, 1999. For me, the anxiety begins in bed, very early in the morning. I'm half awake – I don't want to get up. Did I say the wrong thing to that reporter? Will the students be mad at me forever? Did the emergency meeting get called? Are we prepared to present to the Regents? Did legal counsel ever give us a decision? Why is Mr. X not returning calls? Is today the personnel hearing for grievance #3345, and where is the file?

At this point in their careers, most people have figured it out – it's endless and you can work 24/7, but you need rest, reflection, and play time too. A 10-12 hour day is typical, and you work at least one day of the weekend, if not both. Count on lots of evenings and weekends being consumed by university, student, alumni, community and legislative events, fundraising dinners, award luncheons, concerts, sporting events, plays, poetry readings, and much more.

Facing problems and finding solutions are a normal part of the day. On the other hand, a student death, the burning of a residence hall, hate crimes, and student demonstrations usually belong in the category of crisis. In crises, the Vice President of Student Affairs is often at the forefront. As critical as it is to remain calm, it is also vital that you "blame no one and *do something*." A crisis can overwhelm and consume us. *Let it.* Clear your calendar and devote all your energy – and other people's energies – to events at hand.

If you don't have your own standing crisis group, create one. Our Monday morning check-in meetings about student behavior form the basis of our team. The campus police, the communications office, and the Directors of Counseling, Residence Halls, Student Conduct, and Greek Affairs are all present. Started by the interim Vice President before me, this group has effectively coordinated efforts to head-off problems before they explode.

While I would not want to depend on it, I do believe that Student Services professionals equal the campus HAZMAT team for effectiveness in an emergency. We are calm in our quick response, give and take orders well, and we think of everything from coloring books and Band Aids to onsite psychological counselors and phone banks.

We don't merely respond to crises; often, we anticipate them. As I was traveling to NASPA in New Orleans in March 1999, I got an email from Vicky Triponey, who was finishing her first year as Vice President at the University of Connecticut. She wrote to tell me she could only stay until Sunday evening because they anticipated student riots around the NCAA Final Four Tournament.

Back to the everyday. In my first year I went to everything. But I came to realize the value of attending events primarily for my own sake and when my presence is appreciated by others. I still maintain a very active schedule, despite the occasional urge to go home and read a good book.

Something Better About April

March 30, 1999. Being a Vice President at a mid-sized land grant institution is hard work! I love it. I can do it fairly well and better as time goes by. But phew! Intense stuff – politics, legislation, student issues, staff issues, a growth initiative, struggles between northern and southern Nevada for money, being assertive, not losing one's cool, getting a handle on my budget, bleeding along with academics, communicating with everyone, keeping morale high, showing support by showing up, finding time for me – just relaxing, being quiet, lying on the couch, watching TV, reading a book…oh well, I never really did much of that anyway.

March did, in fact, go out like a lamb. If the month was full of worry, anxiety, and being overwhelmed, by the beginning of April I got hold of things.

It was clear that I not only had to be organized but *highly* organized, with a system of notebooks and files that worked for me and not the system I had inherited from others. Two full weekends alone in the office, and I finally had everything where I could lay my hands on it.

I had to demand more time to do work in my office and began cooperating more effectively with the administrative assistant who kept my calendar. I also started to delegate in new ways. I was pleased when I heard one Director announce to the entire staff, "Everyone knows that when you go to Shannon's office, you leave with ten more things to do."

Spread Your Wings to Help Others Fly

April 6, 1999. I write often about trying to reverse the autocratic way. Some staff love it, others don't, but it is MY way and my confidence in it persists.

Being true to myself, I began working that first spring to create an environment for innovation. Some important ingredients in that process:

- Show up where you are not expected. Go home wonderfully tired – and not from the stresses of budget, personnel, conflicts, and dissension.
- Sit in on faculty senate meetings even when you aren't scheduled to speak.
- Attend every student government meeting you can and simply listen.
- Arrive at the neighborhood meeting with good news. The element of surprise is not to be underestimated.

- While you are at it, ask people what they would do if they could wave a magic wand. The dreams that get lost in the daily shuffle will begin to emerge. It's exciting to watch.

I'd Rather Be Building Trust

April 27, 1999. The Director of Residential Life comes by with good news/bad news. We are already overbooked. We have not reached this point until August 15 in years past. Residential Life is in a panic, yet they are also thrilled.

Unless you are a former housing officer who had the opportunity to build a residence hall or the lucky Union Director who got to build the dream student union, then you have little experience in this field. Trust me, it would help to have some.

Remember my first day? The university architect came to tell me I needed to ask the President for $350,000 more for a new dining services ventilation system that would not block the English department's view. I asked a lot of questions and then told him he needed to make it work without the extra dollars. When we finally got the amount down to $250,000, the President just laughed and said it was worth it to him to not hear the faculty complain.

In hindsight, I should have learned a lesson: When somebody else is spending our money it can only lead to no good.

A strong partnership between the community, the facilities professionals on campus, and Student Services built a beautiful residence hall for 259 students in only 10 months. In the process, I learned lessons about zealous concrete pourers and architects who thought this was to be the Taj Mahal. The amount in contention rose to $1 million, but after the finger pointing was over, we divided up the difference and parted as friends.

I hoped we would never have to build another building. But this is fast-growing Nevada, and two years later I was back in the same soap opera. A donor was secured for a new Student Services building, but the excavated site sat dormant for a year. Finally the Development Vice President and I pressed jointly and ground was broken three weeks later.

Relationships were rocky with both the facilities folks and the contractor. We negotiated up front with our facilities people, got everything in writing, and brought the Vice President who oversees facilities into every meeting. We reported on fiscal status and physical progress to the President's Council on a regular basis. Our Student

Services staff did their best, but they are not construction supervisors.

An SSAO colleague at another Nevada university wisely hires an experienced construction consultant, who oversees the project from a Student Services perspective and handles all the cantankerous issues and keeps everything in line.

Perhaps it is a sign of the economic times, but I am approached at least five times a year from groups seeking to build housing for us, usually using our tax-exempt bonding capacity. Some are local, many are not; a few have land to offer, but most do not. Everybody needs us to guarantee priority in the housing assignment process. Some will give us the building immediately upon completion and others after 30 years. No one wants to run the facility; everyone will gladly turn that over to the University.

Don't get me wrong. I am not against private developer partnerships for housing. I used to be, but like many, I have come to see their value, especially when you have run out of money or land. Colleagues are happier with the partnership when the University, not the developer, crafts the RFP; quality is not sacrificed and there are fewer complaints.

One last important note. You have to work with these people over and over again. Many building projects will come your way during a vice presidency. Some you actually plan for and many you do not. Whatever the tensions, you have to find a reasonable way to talk it out and work it out. There will be another project and their goodwill and expertise will help you accomplish your vision.

Everything I Needed to Know I Learned at Entry Level

May 18, 1999. Commencement. My first complete academic year. I feel I accomplished much and, at the same time, very little. I broadcast a "thank you" e-mail to the Division – I can always be more of a cheerleader.

In some ways, five years as a fraternity/sorority advisor with two different Greek systems had already toughened my skin, broadened my shoulders, shrunk my tear ducts, and exposed me to everything imaginable to prepare me for the life of a new Vice President. I am certain the same could be said for resident advisors and front-line student activities staff.

I may not have had a brilliant insight at the end of year one, but I can share a few lessons with those new to our profession:

- Always let your supervisor know before he or she finds it out from someone else or reads it in the paper.

- Be nice to everyone, since anyone may be your boss some day.
- Keep your shoes polished, mentor many, and when in doubt wear a black suit.
- Never order French onion soup at a business dinner.
- No one wants to hear your whining.
- Participate in the retirement plan, no matter what the financial strain.
- Proofread everything for accuracy and typos and then proofread it again.
- Be honest and be optimistic, especially when things look their worst.
- Keep students at the forefront of it ALL.
- What you are worrying about today will be replaced by a new worry next week, and you will find it hard to remember last week's problem.
- Trust is hard won and easily lost.
- Laugh a lot.
- Learn, learn, learn; you will never know it all.
- Someone with courage is never a failure.
- Waking up at 3 a.m. is an occupational hazard.
- Everything is politics.
- Follow the money.
- Apply the same advice to yourself that you wisely dispense to students.
- Your parents will never understand what you do for a living.
- Find passion and reward in your daily work.

And be thankful that you found a profession where you change lives – every day.

Remembering One Who Pushed

August 18, 1999. A tragic accident ends Dick Stenard's life all too early and devastates hundreds of Student Affairs colleagues around the country. Today we come together in disbelief at the memorial in La Grande, Oregon, crying, commiserating, and eventually telling wonderful and funny stories.

My dear friend, mentor, and NASPA colleague Dick Stenard died on August 12, almost to the day of my one-year anniversary as a Vice President for Student Services. Dick was the Vice President for Student Affairs at Eastern Oregon University and had been NASPA's Region Five Vice President and candidate for NASPA President.

Of the hundreds of memories I have of Dick, the one most with me is his firm gentleness. He was always pushing me and many of my colleagues. He would call and say, "It's time, Shannon. You need to run for NASPA Regional Vice President." He would catch me in the Regional Suite: "It's time, Shannon. Go become a Vice President at a school."

Dick did this for many of us in the field, whether we worked for him or not. That was Dick, pushing us gently into the next leadership role, the next scary place, the next level up. In his memory I have adopted this trait and hope it has helped someone else to gain the confidence and courage to become a Vice President for Student Services.

3. Being Myself

Discovering Difference

August 16, 1998. First week on the job and I am already working closely with Division staff to go beyond rhetoric and develop a 21-point action plan to create an inclusive campus environment. This passion I have about diversity – where did that come from?

I was raised by highly educated teacher parents in Barrington, Illinois, a white suburb of Chicago. My exposure to people of color and other cultures was very limited: a third grade teacher from Hawaii who did not stay long, a family in the neighborhood that seemed darker skinned than us. College in the 1970s did not offer much more to my cultural education. I was, I'm afraid, your typical white student, critical of black students for living in one set of residence halls and of international students for sitting apart in the cafeteria.

Truth be told, I was probably very scared, and if one of these students had said one word to me, I would probably have jumped out of my white skin in fear. Fear of what, I haven't the faintest idea.

But then I took a job in the big city of Los Angeles, and worked and lived side-by-side with people of every race, religion, nationality, sexual orientation, socioeconomic class, and disability. People who lived with bars on their windows and others in stylish apartments in West Hollywood. It was reality and it was my educational haven. People took the time and had the patience to teach me a million valuable lessons about diversity, inclusion, difference, and similarity. I confronted my fears and ignorance, my own "isms." My teachers were gentle and merciless, steadily confronting, reflecting, prodding, joking, soothing – but always teaching.

These life-changing experiences transferred easily when I moved to the Pacific Northwest, where my education on Native American cultures intensified, and they have inspired my work throughout my career. By the time I arrived in Reno, Nevada, I was deeply committed to working and educating in a multicultural environment – wonderfully rich in difference and full of tension and celebration.

Cue, Please?

October 14, 1998. I have a great phone conversation with former NASPA President Jack Warner. He asks how it is going and I tell him that, frankly, the adjustment to "acting like a Vice President" is pretty difficult.

I tend to be fairly loud and outspoken, enjoy a spirited argument, and love to laugh. As a new Vice President, I found myself trying to be quieter, more of a questioner and a listener, and needing to clarify when I was sharing an opinion and when I was issuing a specific direction. I told Jack that I noticed how discussions in the office often ended when I launched an opinion into the fray, sometimes simply when I walked into the room.

"It's like they want me to act a certain way."

He laughed. "You mean they want you to act like a Vice President?"

"Exactly," I said. "I don't want to come off as if I am better than everyone else. I don't want to be seen as different."

Jack's wise advice has never left me. He said, "Shannon, they want you – they need you – to act like a Vice President, their leader. They want to be proud of you. They want you to command the respect of the President and the Regents, the other Vice Presidents and the Deans. They want to respect you themselves."

Lights, Camera, Action!

August 26, 1998. I give my first real speech to the whole Division. I feel overwhelmed with confidence and excitement about what we can do. Some of the staff appear to be overwhelmed, period.

When I look back over the speeches from early in my vice presidency, they sometimes seem a bit pompous, straining a little too much. But it's like watching an old home movie: some parts make me squirm, but mostly I also can laugh and recognize that this is who I was then and still am now.

Here is what I told the staff that day:

"So you've read my resume and shared a bagel with me this morning. "Okay, she's friendly enough," you think to yourself. "But who is she really? What kind of Vice President will she be? What kind of leader? Advocate? Supervisor?"

"I'll answer that this way. Remember this about me: I am very clear about who I am and what I stand for. I know why I chose to come here. I believe I have found a place where I can be myself and pursue the things I think are most important to our students, faculty, staff, and community members. No matter what you do in this Division you need to know that I strive to be honest and hardworking. I will ask of you only those things that I too am willing to do.

"I don't eat lunch. I believe strongly in the need to recruit and retain underrepresented populations in higher education. This means we need to look more diverse and act in full awareness of and with respect for difference. I love to be in conversations where we honestly disagree. I can be persuaded by data. I don't believe alcohol has any relevance on today's college campus. I think dissension is the soul of higher education and out of difficult dialogues comes deep learning. This also causes me headaches, sleepless nights, and cancelled vacations.

"I have never believed that Student Services was a second class citizen to academics on campus and I will not work with people who believe this. We are partners – no better and no worse – in helping students learn. Students are many things and one of those things is a customer. They deserve first-rate service all the time. No, they are not always right.

"I am caffeine dependent, an eternal optimist, and sometimes direct to a fault. I am not very compassionate, but I'm working on it. I despise 'boss tosses.'

"I fully expect you to take things off my plate, not pile them on. I love bread like some people love chocolate. It is an honor and privilege to work in this profession. If you disagree, do us all a favor and go work someplace else. We've got important things to do and I need passionate and committed people to help do this work."

The Power of "Nice"

My relationships with the Assistant Vice Presidents and Directors have changed over time. Like marriages, they require a lot of hard work – time together, time apart, honest communication, realistic limits, and dreaming together.

As an administrator and leader, I believe a critical role is as a builder of bridges – always and forever creating open lines of communication, tending to relationships, and treating people the way we want to be treated. When I fail in crafting a new policy, revising an old process, transforming behavior, or changing attitudes, it is often because I have not obeyed my own insights and advice.

Life and work are ever-changing. Your ability to "be nice" is a great advantage, especially when others are being cruel and unfair. As they sink deeper into their anger, they become more isolated and less articulate, they lose perspective and grow less effective. Your ability to reach them and keep communication going is important. It will be a lifeline for them when everyone else has walked away.

Someday they will need you. For some SSAOs it is Athletics, for others it is the Senior Budget Officer. In bad years it is the student government or another student constituency that does not feel heard. Be there for them, despite the fact that you have every right to walk away. Never, ever give up. As they are forced to exchange ideas and emotions, they will eventually arrive at solutions.

Making the Role My Own

December 15, 1998. I have been asking staff how they are doing with my style. This doesn't mean I will change it but it does mean I want to help them adjust to me. After many astonished looks I am getting valuable feedback.

I've known Vice Presidents who never answer their phone or make photocopies; one only met staff by appointment and rarely interacted with students. A friend of mine in career development said her boss had never set foot in the placement center during 10 years on the job. Everyone's personality and situation is different, and I cannot judge other senior officers. But hearing such stories, I always knew that this was not the kind of Vice President I wanted to be; it was certainly not the kind of Dean, Assistant Vice President, or Director I had been.

But what kind of Vice President *did* I want to be?

Most important, I wanted to be an advocate for students. I often say that if no one else "at the president's table" thinks about students, I must be the one to ask: "How is this in the best interest of our students?" I should also be the one experienced enough to accept, refine, or reject the answer to that question.

As the years have gone by, I have added to my responsibilities helping my vice presidential colleagues, Academic Deans, and Presidents ask the question before I even have to raise it. Nothing makes me happier than when the Vice President for Research or Development asks a student-centered question before I do.

I also knew I wanted to be the kind of Vice President who takes criticism well. Now, I'll be honest here. I do not really like criticism, especially about something in which I am heavily invested. A speaker once suggested viewing criticism as a gift. "When someone is criticizing you," she said, "pretend that they have put a beautiful gift on a silver platter and they are presenting it to you. You smile and take the gift in a gracious manner." I have used this visual more than once and it helps me to keep myself in check, to not allow my buttons to be pushed, to truly *hear* the criticism and mull it over.

Often, despite its sting, criticism is just and it is essential that I hear it. I value being accessible to anyone who needs me. So I was taken aback when, 10 months into the job, a staff member told me he had heard others in the Division say that I had been "scarce" lately, that early in my vice presidency I had been around quite a bit but recently they had not seen me at all. My first reaction was defensive: "Oh no, I've been in all the offices, they just haven't been there when I was." But luckily I saw that silver platter coming and I stopped myself. I asked him to tell me more and as he elaborated the gift became clear. He said "People feel good when you come by to see them. They appreciate the time and care you take. They like you, Shannon."

Needless to say, whether it was true or not, I became very conscientious about getting out of my office and going over to others'. I also learned to leave small notes on desks to let staff know I had dropped in just to say hello or find out how things were going.

Fashion Tips for the New VP

March 12, 1999. I am tired and exasperated. I have had double appointments back-to-back, evening commitments, midnight to 4 a.m. for paperwork and writing the next day's speeches and presentations. I admit it: I'm frazzled!

Trust me, in your first year you do not have time to worry about fashion, much less mow the lawn, build or buy a house, housebreak a puppy, or send holiday cards.

Invest in a few good black and navy suits. They will save you in a wide variety of events, including board meetings, legislative hearings, banquets, award ceremonies, concerts, plays, last-minute business dinners, impromptu speeches. When you have no idea what to wear, they work.

Make sure you have a year's supply of clothes, kiss your family and pets goodbye, and program the VCR. You life will be devoted, appropriately, to learning by listening, by asking, and most of all by doing. The duties of the Vice President don't stop until you or others in your life are ready to stop. You have to hit the ground running. They have been waiting for you!

Those Were the Days – But So Are These

January 6, 1999. I admit there are times when I look at the close friendships among some staff and get nostalgic for when I had the same camaraderie with my Student Affairs colleagues. In fact, some of our fun derived from talking about the Vice President!

I came to realize that I was not and never would be "one of the gang." Colleagues in and out of Student Services are friendly and we occasionally have lunch, spend free time together on business trips, and socialize a little. But no matter how close we get, I am always the Vice President. Even casual conversations are always considered official and I find myself taking great care to not appear as favoring one staff member over another.

It's okay if they talk about me. I hope I prove to be a source of interest and even amusement from time to time. But I miss the friendship and have luckily found it with others outside my Division and University. My best friend of all continues to be my husband, who could write his own book about being married to a new Senior Student Affairs Officer!

Enter the Boomers

March 12, 1999. Is it possible that I represent the next generation of SSAOs? With all the retirements going on there appears to be a significant leadership transition. It is as if the profession sheds its skin every 15 or 20 years, like a snake.

When a generational shift occurs it can often be a time to throw out the old manuals of operation and look for different ways to lead. As a new

SSAO, I do not think I am alone in trying to assess what to retain from the past and what to create for the future.

The baby boom generation is the new voice of Student Affairs leadership on campus and in the profession. In his book *Generations: The History of America's Future, 1584 to 2069*, Neil Howe predicts that new leadership will peak around 2006 and last until 2010 or longer. Individuals with dynamic personalities will most likely rise to the top, but crossing the line into charisma will be a detriment, however, since trust of leaders seems more fragile than ever – and more important than ever.

Howe writes that we boomers fixate on values and we like truth. Perhaps the most significant contribution to cultivating trust is, quite simply, to tell the truth. But *how* you do so is critical. I know that in the past year I've erred at times by being either boring or overly dramatic when trying to be honest. Understating budget constraints and overstating budget cuts do not deliver the best message. I don't want people to panic, but I want them to understand the severity of certain situations, and this requires a tempered approach to sharing hard facts, which I've also tried to develop among the senior staff officers.

A Word About "The Gender Thing"

March 13, 1999. Although our profession may seem overrun by women (not necessarily a bad thing), I find myself immersed in a culture dominated by males. In a room full of men, some will stare at me, waiting for – what? Permission to speak, I conclude. Whether I give it or not, I prepare for the worst.

Once a Dean was telling the staff about a graduate student who had sex with an instructor and later claimed to have been "violated." With a smirk, he made it clear that he could say more if I weren't present. That old conversation-stopper came to mind: "When will you guys learn not to dip your pen in the company ink?" I said it, and it worked.

Another time, the campus architect was dismissing the complaints of the women's center staff that the 10-year master plan omitted their building. "Where's the men's center?" he asked me, to a chorus of snickers. I replied: "Look all around you – since 1874, it's been the whole campus, the whole city, this country, the world!" He paused, and then admitted, "I guess that was a chauvinistic comment." I said, "Yep, and I haven't heard one for about an hour." Big laughs….

My first year, I was the only woman Vice President and, aside from the President's assistant, the only female in cabinet meetings. It was a familiar feeling, since I had been the only woman on the Student Services leadership team at my previous institution. To be honest, I rarely think about the gender mix.

While much has been written about female versus male styles of leadership, I am not completely convinced that differences exist. Jim Collins wrote an article in the *Harvard Business Review* about "Level Five Leadership." The leaders profiled in the article – all men – are praised for leading good-to-great transformations of their organizations due to a blend of extreme personal humility with intense professional will. I think many women, including myself, have been combining these two seemingly opposite traits with incredible success for many, many decades, if not centuries.

Forget the Odds, Just Bet on Yourself

May 28, 1999. I am so honored to give the keynote to Seattle University's spring graduates in Student Development Administration. All were students of mine in the program's introductory course, and it was great fun to see them again, to celebrate their accomplishment, and to share some advice.

I am often asked the question, "What's the coolest thing about being a Vice President for Student Affairs?" My answer might be one of the pieces of advice I gave in that Seattle speech: "Remember to bend the rules once in a while and when you reach a point in your career where your job is to make those rules, try to get rid of a few of the dumb ones."

I have truly never felt more capable of bringing about change – transforming the institution to create a learning community with clear values and expectations and taking action on those beliefs. These are not platitudes. They are my professional values, my personal values, which I believe in so strongly that sometimes I scare myself.

Robert Jarvik, inventor of the Jarvik-7 artificial heart, wrote that "leaders are visionaries with a poorly developed sense of fear and no concept of the odds against them." Courage and selective ignorance have made me wise and forward thinking in more than one presidential council meeting, academic retreat, or system meeting.

Hopefully those moments of insight, innovation, and wisdom outweigh the times I looked stupid. Suppressing your creative and even outlandish thoughts reduces you to something you were not meant to be, denies your campus the glow of your talents and the rewards of your heartfelt passion, and deprives us all of the kind of leaders we desperately need.

4. Managing Student Services

Who's in Charge Here?

August 15, 1998. I've been out eavesdropping. I walk and walk around campus, trying to get a feel for how people experience the University.

By September it was clear that I had to focus energies on changing the culture that allowed – no, *expected* – the Vice President to make all the decisions. I felt that this was unhealthy and unwise. It is very useful to get out of my office and travel the campus widely, listen carefully, and look for patterns.

In my first six weeks I saw multiple examples of no ownership – no deep thinking about ramifications. It wasn't that people lacked the talent, knowledge, and ability. What, I wondered, was holding them back?

A Quick Win – Part One

August 21, 1998. Years ago, a supervisor told me that, as his new hire, I needed a "quick win," something visible and long desired by the staff or students that would convey the message that I could get things done. Find something you want to do, he said, and I will help you accomplish it. Once again I have found something.

The President wanted to promise the chancellor 3% growth in the fall. I told him I couldn't get us there in two months, but I could begin mobilizing the troops. The excellent admissions staff was hard working but weary. Becoming the center of attention revitalized them. A multitude of others also wanted to help in Academic, Administration, Finance, Development, and Student Service departments. Everyone joined together with a new sense of commitment.

We started with a quick assessment: What academic and student services programs for recruitment and retention were working the most effectively? We turned out a publication on best practices and distributed it widely across the University. This gave recognition where it was due and provided models for others to adopt.

I listened hard to staff, faculty, and students. What did they want to do, and how could I help make it happen? What barriers could I remove? Many staff responded immediately:

"I've always wanted new student orientation to last longer."

"I've wanted a traditional opening ceremony full of inspiring celebration for new students."

"I'd like to stop allowing community college students to live in our residence halls."

"I'd like to teach."

"I want to create a culturally sensitive leadership development class."

"I want to create a program to help new students who are 'at risk' succeed."

"We need a GLBT Student Center."

"I want to attract more Native American students to the University."

"Can all the building signs be in Spanish as well as English?"

"Let's make volunteering in the community a requirement."

"Let's require one semester of study abroad."

"We need to get rid of teaching placement files."

And on and on. A reflective minority needed time to think, but they eventually came back – in some cases, years later – with wish lists.

My quick win became their dreams. No single project cost more than a few thousand dollars. The approval, support, cheerleading, and seed money created hope, which generated enthusiasm, which became momentum that gathered energy in the coffee line and spread throughout the Division. We were moving, changing, shaking ourselves and others, awakening and embracing optimism and possibilities on a daily basis.

Were there naysayers? You bet. I let them remain so.

Were there curious onlookers? Absolutely. They only needed coaxing and, at times, a little push from trusted colleagues.

Were other divisions making fun of us? Perhaps, but when I asked them to join us in innovative summits and problem-solving dialogues, they were first at the table. The student services staff sometimes wondered if those offices had become a part of our Division.

Ready, Set, Reorganize

August 23, 1998. I have not been here two weeks and people are already asking when I'm going to reorganize.

It is not uncommon for a new Vice President to be confronted with a multitude of requests to spend money, change people's duties or reporting lines, and commit to long-term goals before you are ready. Structuring your division is one of the central issues facing any Vice President. It is more than an organizational chart with lines, boxes, and titles. Bolman and Deal put it succinctly, saying, "It is a depiction of the formalized pattern of activities, expectations, and exchanges among individuals." We all know the positive and negative power of structure on the accomplishments and attitudes of staff.

Do not be hurried. Your staff members are a precious resource, and you should settle upon roles and relationships that will further the strategic goals of your division and institution. I also caution you not to take too long. Sometimes you just know the right thing to do. I suspect I did. Most people expected significant changes in the first year and told me so. I took it as a sign that the time was right. Our strategic plan also pointed to change along the lines everyone seemed to want. Once the reorganization was announced, I often heard, "Well, it's about time."

We were not as concerned with vertical strategies as with coordination. Problem solving and big new initiatives could be helped along by pulling together the right departments and experienced people into long-term, sustainable relationships. While there may be no best way to organize, some ways are better than others.

For example, our residential life and dining staff were experts at value engineering and could build expansive new facilities. Our goal of building a new student union required the two staffs to collaborate. We made that easier by putting both units under one Associate Vice President. More recently, we got a chance to combine our offices serving under-represented populations under one Assistant Vice President. From their first meetings together, the synergy was apparent.

Say It with Doughnuts

August 24, 1998. First day of classes. I take a dozen doughnuts to the Financial Aid office to thank them for their tireless efforts. You would think I had brought them gold. We schmooze a little before everyone heads off to meetings. I do the same in Residential Life and Orientation offices.

Four years later I still hear about those doughnuts. Staff tells me that whenever they think they feel unappreciated or misunderstood, they remind one another of "the doughnuts." I'm still doing it, every year, and it still makes everyone feel good – including me.

I Inherit a Fortune

September 12, 1998. Sometimes, I just stop and count my blessings.

To be a successful Vice President for Student Services, there is an essential ingredient over which you must have some control. I was fortunate enough to inherit this vital component: four staff members who reported directly to me – three Assistant Vice Presidents and an administrative assistant. All had been at the University a long time and contributed to my immediate successes. They continue to be critical to all that we have accomplished in Student Services. Pardon the cliché, but I could not have done it without them.

Each of the Assistant Vice Presidents should be a Vice President for Student Services at a college or university. They each have their own reasons for remaining in Reno. Their ideas and actions, risks and rollicking laughter, their ability to stay calm in a crisis, to make fun of themselves, to take on the unexpected, to create chaos and find success in ambiguity, and to lead with passion are evident in our team.

Some colleagues are shocked that there are three Assistant Vice Presidents in my Division. They ask, "Aren't you worried that you look too top heavy?" I tell them that I have three capable and respected leaders who triple our effectiveness as a Division. This "depth on the bench" allows us to be everywhere we need to be – from student meetings to venues where policy decisions must be made. The three of them have the power and knowledge to take action and make commitments.

Others ask if I regret not being able to make my own hires. I firmly answer, "No regrets." Their historical knowledge and wisdom is a welcome addition to every conversation, as is their willingness to try new things and create change. But many new Vice Presidents will inherit staff who are underperforming or cannot participate in a new vision. When the transformation in attitude and action does not occur in a reasonable period of time you must, for your own sake, bring about change. Often this "last resort" can be avoided by months of conversations with staff about what you expect from them, including clear feedback on their performance. When enough time has passed, you have *got* to be selfish. Help these people find other jobs and hire new people who will help you achieve your goals.

The shoe was on the other foot when the President who hired me left and a new one arrived. He inherited me! I wanted to be as valuable to him as the senior Student Services staff was to me when I arrived on the job. It was a challenge figuring out his style, how he dealt with negative feedback, and what he thought of students and Student Services. To put it mildly, his first year was a wild ride.

More than once in my fourth year at the University – my first with the new President – I came back from a meeting and apologized to the administrative assistant for what I must have certainly said or done in my first year. In wanting to improve things for the future, I am sure I came off as critical of those before me. In wanting to reorganize and restructure, I am sure I sometimes looked ignorant. In wanting to make my mark quickly, I sometimes erased the marks made by others in the past.

No Questions Asked

October 1, 1998. I seem to have a new relationship with power.

In several of my earliest journal entries, I register surprise over my newfound power as Vice President. I never expected experiences like the ones I had, and it took a while to get used to them.

On my first day, a young woman came by the office when I was the only one there. She had a financial problem, so I called the Student Financial Services office to ask a question about her financial aid package – only a factual question, mind you, not a request and certainly not an order. My mere inquiry immediately brought changes in her favor.

The next day, another student came in who had been working with the previous Vice President. She told me she had been sexually assaulted the previous year, left school, and was now trying to come back. An outstanding debt associated with her abrupt withdrawal, kept her from registering. I told her to call back in an hour. In the meantime, I made a number of calls to the cashier's office and the registrar that eventually resulted in cancellation of the debt so she could enroll. While this was certainly the outcome I desired, I was uneasy that I had not waited to consult with the Assistant Vice President who oversees such things. When we did connect, she concurred with the outcome and was slightly amused with my concern over "doing her job." In her easygoing style, she said I could feel free to do that anytime.

What was this new job of mine? In mere conversations regarding students' situations, I was never questioned. My inquiries were taken as requests, and I got what I wanted. I kept saying "Wait, first tell me if this is going by the rules." But things kept getting taken care of. While I am confident that we acted in the best interest of the students, I made a vow not to use power in that way again. I should have passed the problems back to staff who handle these situations as part of their job and have a process to follow.

No Questions Asked (Reprise)

I stuck to that promise, except once. At our University, salary adjustments, promotions, and new titles are granted by a committee of six upper-level individuals who report directly to Vice Presidents in Student Services, Academics, and Administration and Finance. They meet in closed-door sessions and are perceived as wielding much power.

Time and again, I would send forward solid cases for promotion, with supporting documentation, and they would be denied. My Student Services representative on the committee finally told me that other VPs bypass the committee and go directly to the President. I admit that I gave in and did just that with the next big promotion. The President called me in to discuss it and said that another Vice President objected. I found this interesting, since the committee's deliberations were supposed to be confidential. I stated my case, and the next day the promotion was approved.

Our representative on the committee reported that at the next week's meeting the chair mentioned (just "FYI") that the Student Services promotion had received presidential approval. There were some raised eyebrows and questions were asked, but the chair simply said, "It was approved by the President."

Had other Vice Presidents not bypassed the process? Yes, but not I. Did anyone wonder what drove me to such desperation? No. They were just mad that I went around them. Did they ever get mad at the other Vice Presidents? No, they were used to that behavior from them. For a moment, I was glad to be in the same league as the other conniving and "political" Vice Presidents. I had won something for my Division.

I felt lousy.

Office of ... What?

October 15, 1998. One of the things that always bothered me about services for students was some of the names we gave them. Student Success, TRIO, Student Life. If I am a student, what do those programs offer me?

I surely can't tell by the title. They may not be fancy, but Tutoring Services, Counseling Center, Student Activities, and Career Services are pretty clear to me and the thousands of students who use them. Do them a favor and, in your first year, label things clearly so they are understandable and user friendly.

I Repeat, Who's in Charge Here?

November 21, 1998. I truly am shocked at having so many good people give up so much intelligence, wisdom, and authority to me. To their shock, I am turning it back.

In my first meetings with Student Services staff I was asked to "share my vision." People actually picked up their pens, pulled out pads of paper and sat poised with hands ready to take down, as one Director stated, "our marching orders."

While I had a sense of the kind of Student Services Division I wanted to lead, I knew that a key ingredient was my staff's ability to innovate, create, and implement programs and services that would help students have an excellent experience. My staff needed to understand that their ideas and aspirations mattered. For my part, I needed to coach and develop the staff so that they would free my time for things that only the Vice President should deal with. This goes beyond delegating. It is about changing the Student Services culture.

When I explained this at our opening sessions, most looked at me with a confused, even deflated look. I remember saying, "I'll bet each and every one of you has wanted to try something on the job and for whatever reason you haven't been able to do it. You need money, you need to make the time, you need to cultivate a skill…. If you think a minute, I'll bet you can come up with something you want to do to promote student success at Nevada. THAT is a central part of my vision. MY job is to remove the barriers, find the resources, and support you in achieving these things."

Innovating is one thing, but creating a climate of self-confidence is harder. Simply turning decisions back to staff was not enough. I learned that I needed, first, to talk over with them the possibilities and the best process to follow. Second, I needed to reassure them of my complete support in whatever they decided. That part was harder. During most of the year, staff would come to me and ask if I really meant it when I said I would support them in their decisions. In time, they learned.

One of my greatest contributions was to pinpoint the urgency or the lack of urgency of decisions. Most often I find myself playing the role of slowing things down. Time brings cooler heads, reflective thinking, space for consultation with stakeholders, consideration of all the options, and most often much better decisions. In my younger days it used to frustrate me when the Vice President didn't make decisions quickly. I now have understanding that comes with the wisdom of experience and age. "Slowing down" is a trait of a good leader. This was recently verified in the most pragmatic of ways by University of Southern California President Steven Sample in his 2002 best-selling book, *The Contrarian's Guide to Leadership*. His advice is, "Never make a decision today that you can reasonably put off till tomorrow."

Technology Wrangling

December 5, 1998. I did not "do" technology, beyond Word documents, e-mail, and the occasional spreadsheet. Now, I am bombarded with requests for funds to hire web masters, buy new servers, and purchase multimillion-dollar software. Where is the techie?

Managing the enthusiasm and frustration around technology was one of my earliest challenges. Did Student Services have its own "techie?" No. What information technology infrastructure existed for the University? Not much. I felt doomed.

So I went to school. I quickly learned that I could design a web page in the same time it took to design an old-fashioned brochure. If I could do it, so could everyone else. I redirected my "griping time" into free classes offered by the University. I came to understand servers and portals, Moore's Law (the computing power of a semiconductor chip doubles approximately every 18 months), and the fact that our students fully expected it all to be on the Internet. The more complicated issues, I happily found out, were complicated for everyone. So I called on colleagues, attended conferences, found best practices, and began to develop a core of non-technical administrators who knew how to think, read, analyze, and make decisions.

I was convinced that the only bad course of action would be to ignore technology. Earlier in the year, I had found pockets of technical capability – data warehouses and technical staff in various departments of the Division. I knew we needed a coordinated approach with a shared vision. I'll admit this was hard to come by, as staff had been operating in anonymity and were protective of their turf. More than once I had to remind them that this was not *their* data or *their* money.

Once we caught our breath, we began enjoying the benefits that technology could deliver to our students. I began to view technology not as an expense, but as an investment in which everyone should share (I sell this message at a lot of meetings). It turned out that the hard issues were not the products, but rather staffing and policy. My staff and I continually wrestle with criticisms of unfairness – limited access to technology among less fortunate students – and perceptions of technology as a black hole sucking in dollars better directed elsewhere.

I have learned that technology is one function I cannot delegate. In my first year, I began developing a Division infrastructure with policy and people, hardware and software, that was coordinated and effective. It has taken understanding, knowledge, and expertise in the subject matter, fiscal impact, and investment potential of technology – also, the resistance factions, strategies for effective placement and use, and measurement of success and shortfalls.

My advice on wrangling technology: Ask a lot of questions – dumb questions – and keep your eye on the goal of serving students who are pursuing a higher education. We still face challenges: how best to collaborate with the instructional technology people; how to keep up with a rapidly evolving field; how to envision the future; and, of course, resource planning and ongoing implementation. But, increasingly, we can measure the payoff in terms of student satisfaction, staff morale, and productivity.

A Quick Win – Part Two

February 12, 1999. Everyone has homework assignments, many involving people with whom we have never worked. The Business Dean and the Student Programming Chair are identifying barriers to enrollment. The Vice President for Development, the Budget Analyst, and the State Demographer are comparing school district enrollment projections with economic data. The Vice Presidents for Finance and Academic Affairs are preparing a list of tasks we can accomplish by summer. It all would seem impossible, if we weren't having fun.

My quick win had a lot going for it. Increasing enrollment required a visible collaboration among student services, academic affairs, and finance and administration. We became known as the "Growth Group." Established in January of 1999, our group of Vice Presidents, Deans, and student leaders met on a weekly basis. First, we agreed upon the optimal outcome and then we spent the next three months creating our future – like Merlin – by working back into the past.

(To refresh your memory, Merlin was the mythical wizard in King Arthur's court who was born in the future – and as a result was able to give the King quite useful advice – and aged as he went backwards in time. Charles Smith introduced the Merlin Factor in organizational planning in the 1990s.)

The "Growth Group" put itself into the future by envisioning a 6% enrollment increase by the fall of 2000. We then bantered about programs, initiatives, scholarships, and demographics that would all need to be aligned by then. We met in the student senate chambers with shirtsleeves rolled up. Sometimes, we called our secretaries to cancel all our meetings for the rest of the day because we were on a roll.

Maybe Someone IS in Charge

April 8, 1999. "It is ultimately your decision." I hear this all the time. It is as if they saved up every decision for the moment I would arrive on campus.

From my first day as Vice President, I have been asked to make decisions about budget, hiring, firing, space, agendas, salaries, timelines, goals, vision, committee assignments, titles, organizational structure – everything. The very able interim Vice President had made a number of great decisions, moving the Division forward. There were, however, hidden agendas to many pending decisions put before me and the earlier they came in my tenure the more laden with controversy, historical innuendo, and political pitfalls.

My first afternoon of meetings was "negative, negative," as I wrote in my journal. I met with the Assistant Vice Presidents one by one and heard about budget overruns (or deficits, as some called them) in the second month of the fiscal year. Pressures from the Chancellor to increase enrollment beyond a comfortable 2-3% each year had reached fever pitch, and we were lagging behind. The technological infrastructure was nonexistent, with no hope in sight for any improvement. Surely things could not be all doom and gloom.

They were not. In hindsight I see that this was a venting time for staff. They were also telling me the truth, and nothing came as much of a surprise. I had heard about these things during the interview process.

Now they were my issues as well. I have found that *my* first day was typical. Problems are the food of vice presidents. DO NOT BE SCARED if this happens to you. The fun is working with others to resolve them.

Of course, my first response is to solve them myself, but we all know (don't we?) that this is not a good idea. Fortunately, I can ask questions relentlessly. From the very first day, whenever I was pressed for an answer, I replied with 10 questions. What if? Why not? Why? More information reveals possibilities to me and, more important, to the person presenting the problem. Asking the right questions eventually resolves the problem.

Mother Knows Best

May 8, 1999. Delegating authority isn't enough. To make their decisions stick, people sometimes need a little backup. My mother knew this.

When I was a child, it was my mother's job to provide an excuse for me to not stay for dinner at a friend's house, to avoid a sleepover or birthday party – anything I disliked doing but was afraid or unable to decline. We had a routine. I would call from the friend's house, "They want me to stay for dinner." My mom would ask, "Do you want to stay for dinner?" I'd say no, and she would reply, "Then tell them your mother says you can't stay and you have to come home."

At work, staff will call and say, "So-and-so wants us to pay $12,000 for the University web page." I'll ask, "Do you think we should pay $12,000 for the web page?" They'll say no, and I'll reply, "Tell them the Vice President says we can't pay $12,000 for the web page."

Blissfully Ignorant

May 14, 1999. I find that, under the right conditions, ignorance can make me more efficient.

Ignorance has more going for it than most of us realize. I have come to rely on the knowledge of other people, such as the Director of Residential Life or the Director of Financial Aid, rather than learning it all myself. One colleague likened this to our use of a cell phone. Who can explain how it works? When we turn on the phone we depend on the intelligence of engineers, programmers, and designers. We are "blissfully" ignorant.

As Vice President for Student Services, do not expect to acquire the specialized knowledge of your professionals. Your job is to manage the growing relative ignorance more effectively. Look at it this way: A Vice President's involvement is the last resort. Staff can say, "If we can't come to a resolution the Vice President will have the final say." When two divisions are involved, it is useful to say that both Vice Presidents will have to meet and make the decision. This usually throws the other division into a panic, since they don't want their boss to think they can't resolve problems. Resolutions miraculously occur, and all is fair and just.

Disruptive Innovation: Learn to Love It

June 1, 1999. My goal is to develop a disruption-friendly environment in Student Services by spring.

I first read the theory of disruption in the *Educause Review*. Disruption provides a new perspective and is a dynamic force to bring about the achievements we desire. It allows lean and streamlined initiatives to succeed and forces inefficient and unfocused ideas to die. An SSAO reallocates resources in a never-ending cycle of strengthening well-executed ideas while ending expenditures of wasted resources on weak ones.

Given that I was locked into a strategic plan for two more years, I felt stuck when it came to encouraging innovation and reallocating resources. I started by permitting those who saved money through disruptive innovations to keep the money they saved – for now. It was nothing much, at first. The Enrollment Services Unit stopped sending letters and began using postcards that directed students to web pages and easy-to-follow instructions for accessing personal information. Once student email addresses were assigned even the postcards vanished.

We can all cite routine examples. Replacing desktop computers with laptops costing the same amount led to greater connectivity during travel and when people were at home. Staff spent more time working outside the office, but they didn't have to contend with 200 emails when they returned to their desks. Business did not have to stop while they were away. As people acquired cell phones, the need for private lines disappeared. Graduate students began doing more academic advising and supplemental learning, and less tutoring, and the University not only saved money but improved educational quality. We are eliminating computer labs in the residence halls, because nearly all students bring their own. With the savings on equipment and maintenance, we are building up reserves for our next new hall.

Students often view mandatory fees as disruptions. I enjoy working with students to inform them about the reasons for the fee. I encounter every imaginable reason not to impose the fee, and addressing their objections keeps me honest. I figure if there is nothing standing in the way of a new idea, chances are I'm making the evaluation process too easy, or maybe the idea isn't groundbreaking enough.

Our most dramatic disruptive opportunity in my first year was the Governor's surprise announcement that tobacco settlement money would be used for scholarships to Nevada high school graduates with a 3.0 and above. We had a year to prepare for their arrival, with new financial aid processes, a new residence hall, and expansion of lower-division course offerings. I am convinced that our "disruption-friendly" environment and practice on the small scale allowed us to establish a successful recruitment and retention program for these students.

Heart Power

June 10, 1999. You may cringe when I say that in order for a new SSAO to be effective he or she must understand that tapping into "heart power" is critical. As a hard and fast administrator, however, I say it is this passion that sets you apart and above the rest.

Heart power is passion for our role and its contributions to Student Services and the University. It is also our interest in sparking and flaming the passions that others possess. We do this all the time with students, especially when their family wants them to be one thing and the student wants to pursue something else. Why not do ourselves and our colleagues a favor and follow our own good advice? In his book *Orbiting the Giant Hairball*, Gordon MacKenzie writes, "Passion begets success. Success begets success formula. Success formula begets isolation from passion, vision, and innovation. Isolation begets atrophy, decay, a fading away." Become dependent on the passions of your division, your students, and yourself.

Come to Order

June 30, 1999. When I dig deep enough I find chaos beneath the order. The leader in me wants to let it rage and play itself out, while the manager wants to make it neat and orderly. It is a balancing act.

I must have charged 20 committees in my first year – search committees, personnel committee, professional development committee, studies of this and implementation of that. If committee members had more questions after a meeting than before it, I knew I had failed.

The Vice President for Student Services should create clarity while motivating and inspiring. It is your job to introduce change into the culture long before others do it for you. The sooner you act on what you know to be true – that change is constant – the better you will be at creating and leading a relevant, responsive, and cutting-edge Student Services Division.

I came to learn that it wasn't cheating if I worked on key policies and practices to influence change. I set high expectations and worked the Division circuit to inspire staff. I respectfully but directly confronted old practices and thinking. On the advice of one Assistant Vice President for Student Services, I told staff when I had already made up my mind (no alcohol at events where people under 21 are present) and when I had not (should we become a dry campus?). No point in pretending I did not have strong opinions when I truly did.

Remember, committee work is often an add-on to people's busy jobs. When it lacks focus and direction, they get frustrated and often don't volunteer again. It is important to help your staff make sense out of things.

Write and speak well and often. Hit the key points and repeat them consistently. This may occasionally mean focusing people's attention on only those key items of most importance and not the dozen or so fascinating related topics. Other people love to manage the details long before it is time to go there. At Nevada one of our departed senior administrators spent considerable time (and money) on the color of the walls, carpet in the lobby, and light fixtures. While endearing, he should have been obsessing instead about the more important issues facing his institution. People – and committees – need clarity in order to create accomplishment in the chaos.

Closing Thoughts on Being in Charge

July 15, 1999. I look back on my first meeting with my staff, nearly a year ago. Their first question was, "What is your vision?" My answer: "To work with you to come up with OUR vision."

One of my favorite topics is the budget. There is never enough, we are always destined to go in the red, and no one can reduce his or her budget any further. Yet we always make it to year's end at an even finish, with plenty of money reallocated to needy areas and special initiatives. Everyone reduces budgets under mandates, voluntary reallocation, and necessity.

During the first weeks, I was inundated with requests for money. A critical question to ask staff became, "Is this the thing you want me to go to the mat for?" It helped to provide perspective on the importance of the project and request. It clearly asked the staff to prioritize, since I was not willing to move funds or request additional dollars on a regular basis. It also helped me demonstrate the importance of decisions in the context of the overall game plan. How does this request fit in with our goals and vision? If it doesn't, why is this an exception? How does it help or hinder our progress?

My first year I was working hard to change the culture so that everyone felt able to make good decisions. The Vice President did not have a corner on that market, nor was she the single source of goals, vision, initiatives, and innovations. I spent countless hours meeting with individuals and office staff trying to hear from them what needed to be done. Changes, transformations, new programs, terminations, risks, dreams – they were the stuff of excellent Student Services divisions. Unleashing this force among the staff was a tough challenge. They were genuinely puzzled. They kept pushing back and saying, "You just tell us what to do."

At our first year-end retreat I resorted to a visual exercise where everyone stood in a circle. I asked everyone who had power to step into the circle. Everyone took a step forward. Some did it easily, some forcefully, a few rather timidly, but everyone felt able to change, to initiate, to risk, to decide, to innovate, to resolve, since everyone has the power.

Thinking Big

June 22, 2001. I'm off to Japan, on a second Fulbright administrative grant to study higher education in other countries. It's a mini-sabbatical that takes me out of my comfort zone.

Thinking big leads to more powerful thinking. If you seek bigger and better thinking from yourself, your staff, and your students, you have the beginnings of an exemplary Student Services Division.

Rich Keeling of Keeling Associates convinced me to read outside student affairs and higher education, and I am now a loyal reader of *Fast Company*, *American Demographics*, and *The Onion* online. I scan *National Geographic* in our library, even *American Woodworking*. It is a habit that broadens my awareness of what others are viewing and discussing. *The Economist*, a British magazine on current events, and the Canadian Broadcast Company give me completely different takes on world events and on the United States.

I try to meet people who do not work at the University. On the Southwest Airlines milk run from Reno to Las Vegas, I've talked with construction workers, nuclear engineers, reporters, accountants, casino managers, airline mechanics, and state legislators. What are their stressors? How do they solve problems? What's the best part of their job? Did they go to college? Do they hire our graduates? Do they like their own boss? If so, why? If not, why not? Who was their mentor? What are they reading? I always walk away with new ideas, models, metaphors, and a bigger picture.

The challenge is to get the entire Student Services Division thinking big. I heard a lot of conflicting things in my first year. "We don't meet enough as a Division." "We meet too much." "We should send more emails." "You send too many emails." All coupled with complaints like, "I don't know what's going on around here," "Nobody cares about what I'm doing." So I instituted three meetings a year and one retreat in May devoted to NETMAT, which stands for Nobody Ever Told Me About That. We don't keep NETMAT minutes or post anything on the web. Everyone in the Division is encouraged to come with their announcements, to find out what is going on, share information with colleagues, dispel myths, and correct or confirm rumors. We ask questions and share opinions on anything going on at the University.

We conduct NETMAT and other Division gatherings all over campus. The more remote the better – the Medical School, public TV station, journalism reading room, alumni lounge, new coffeehouse, research lab, the Agriculture Extension Ranch, or theatre-in-the-round. One day, I hope to convene a NETMAT at Wally's Hot Springs in the Sierra Nevada mountains.

I invite "wild cards" to observe and participate in our meetings and planning sessions. Faculty can be the wildest cards of all. One respected (and intimidating) scholar listened intently and finally asked us why we wanted to be educators and not service providers? He thought the important role of Student Services was to be the "front door" to the institution. That was, in his eyes, an essential and unduplicated role. No, we said, we are educators *and* service providers. We must always think big.

5. Connecting with the Faculty

It's a Two-Way Street

October 20, 1998. Does Academics Affairs appreciate the importance of partnering with Student Services? Not yet, but we are working on it.

Student Services professionals understand that our work must be related to the academic mission of the institution. We did not grasp this at all times in our profession's history, but we get it now.

Job descriptions, performance reviews, and funding for new initiatives stress our efforts to promote the academic agenda. Directives from Presidents, Provosts, and SSAOs request and require Student Services Divisions to work "more closely with academics in recruitment, enrollment, and retention services."

Last summer, I was driving with the Provost on a long road trip across Nevada and he mentioned that this expectation met with much support from the University-wide strategic planning committee. I turned to him, "And of course you'll put the reverse statement in every academic strategic planning directive, right?" He looked at me, baffled.

"You know," I continued, "You'll make sure that Academics is instructed to work more closely with Student Services on recruitment and retention, curriculum development, and the development of safe spaces in the classroom." He nodded, "Yes," although I knew his mind was tumbling the idea around.

We were silent for quite a while, driving through sagebrush and mountainous desert. It was the beginning of a provocative conversation that has not yet ended. I hope it never does.

Dancing to the Same Beat

December 12, 1998. End-of-semester pressures and celebrations underscore how much Student Services contributes to the campus-learning environment.

Faculty is typically regarded as the intellectual corpus of the institution, and I won't deny that the "life of the mind" is their passion and life's work. But we in Student Services share that focus. We pride ourselves on creating a community where the exchange of radical, dissenting, and exciting ideas is the standard of the day. Student Services professionals, programs, and services exist to initiate and fuel the dialogue in written and verbal forums.

Bridging the Divide

January 14, 1999. I remember my undergraduate years. Faculty showed up in a hall of 500, delivered lectures, and left the paper grading, seminar leading, and personal interaction with students to their teaching assistants.

Traditional institutions made clear the deep separations between Student Services and Academics in physical layout, practice and process, resource allocation, and philosophy. Yet while I was at The Evergreen State College, I admired the innovative system of interspersing Student Services among Academics throughout the library, seminar, and laboratory buildings. I also had the opportunity to watch faculty – in economics, mathematics, and history – assume Student Affairs responsibilities. Faculty members rotated through administrative positions, providing academic and programming advice and developmental counseling.

Arriving at Nevada, I found that Student Services and faculty had not yet evolved to this stage of cooperation. But with every shared project, we move closer. For example, our Division delivers services directly to faculty, such as grade posting, classroom assignments, and (on the Reno campus) the Degree Audit Reporting System, or DARS, which enables undergraduates to monitor their progress toward meeting degree requirements. Students can see which requirements have been completed and which have not, and which courses can fulfill those unmet requirements.

DARS has had its problems, but the process of fixing them gave us an opportunity to improve relations with faculty. We invested in training and assigned a talented techie as point person to communicate face-to-face with every academic unit. As DARS improved, we saw our interactions with the faculty shift from negative to positive. One small step.

Be Not Afraid

April 27, 1999. What usually scares us? Things we do not know or understand…the weird and different…the mysterious and the mythical.

Faculty used to scare me. Why? I suppose I lacked self-confidence and felt I was not worthy of their time or attention. We internalize the negative messages of others and they become our own.

Most faculty members probably do not think of Student Services at all. That's okay. Our job is not to wait for someone else to make the first move in creating partnerships with academics. Our job is to take the lead.

So many of us work with only the same handful of Student Services–friendly faculty. Why? It is easy, safe, predictable. I often advise students and new professionals to introduce themselves to the most intimidating faculty member on campus. Faculty is usually not nearly as difficult as others might think.

During my first two fall semesters, I arranged to meet one-on-one with every new academic faculty member on campus. I have met with at least one third of our faculty over the past four years. When my NASPA commitments took up all my free time, I farmed out the list of new faculty to the three Assistant Vice Presidents in Student Services, and they helped keep an important outreach tradition going. We now draw upon a long list of faculty for committees, work groups, referrals, and internship sponsors. They refer students to us in droves and use our faculty-friendly services on a regular basis.

In these introductory conversations, I have sat on the only stool in the lab, on a stack of newspapers, on orange 1970s couches, and even on a large boulder. I love going down in the depths of science buildings to little closet offices next to huge laboratories, wending my way through a labyrinth of tiny cubicles stuffed with books by William Shakespeare, Richard Feynman, Sandra Cisneros, and Milton Friedman. I am fascinated by the gemstones, fossils, spectrometers, and periodic tables; they are not of my world but they are of the world of my students.

I am reminded once again what higher education is all about. I see committed young scholars and wise sages grading papers, mentoring students, and even hugging pupils for grasping a long-elusive concept. This is, of course, not enough. But it is an important start.

6. Seeing Through Students' Eyes

They Deserve Your Best

September 12, 1998. I remember what the actor, writer, and director Billy Bob Thornton once told an interviewer: I am always aware that people spend their hard-earned money to see my work.

Maybe it's my midwestern work ethic, but I liked that. I try to remember that every student on my campus very likely saved up, even went into debt, to attend this University. They worked terrible hours at grueling jobs and gave up school activities and time with friends and family so they could go to college.

Many in Nevada are the first in their family to attend college. Either everyone is extremely proud of them and they are role models, or it is quite the opposite and their parents do not understand the value of a college education. Parents may even discourage their children's aspirations. Some of our students have made it here against great odds, both financial and emotional, and may not have had competitive academic preparation. They deserve the very best, on a daily basis.

Time to Bust the Great Myths

October 17, 1998. I go out of my way to create opportunities to spend time with students, especially now that I feel they're all my responsibility.

One of the myths of our profession is that the higher you go in the institution and in Student Services, the less you see of students.

I find that my contacts with students are numerous, deeper, and more meaningful than ever. In the past I had responsibility for Greeks or commuters, students in clubs and organizations, or residence halls. My contact with these students was intense and frequent, but focused.

At Nevada I began to meet with every student group. Each fall and spring I get on the agenda of every club and organization to introduce myself, to share any relevant information for that particular group, and, most of all, to listen. I tailor the message to the group and will sit through the entire meeting to understand their issues and concerns. Often, I don't say a word. Sometimes, I interrupt with suggestions, or even offer money to help fund a good program or idea.

When meeting with groups that promote an agenda outside of the predominant culture, I stress my support for them and my open door should they need assistance. I schedule these groups first, since issues of safety and prejudice are often on their minds, rather than less-pressing concerns such as access to playing fields or complaints about the dining commons.

Caring Is in Our Genes — and Our Deeds

February 10, 1999. It is a dream come true finally to be in a position where I can remove barriers, bend policy, and even get rid of rules that prevent students from having a great learning experience.

Another myth is that Vice Presidents do not need to care all that much about students.

Nobody gets to this position by being insensitive and uncaring toward students. Some of my brightest days are when we can influence policy and loosen regulations so students can pursue their education in a less-than-traditional way.

In 1999, under the careful guidance of our Government Relations Officer, I spent considerable time in the Nevada state legislature helping to craft a scholarship out of tobacco settlement money. Now known as the Millennium Scholarship, it allows Nevada's brighter high school graduates to attend college in the state.

Another success was partnering with colleagues on other Nevada campuses to educate our Regents, and then the state legislature, on the increasing number of students with disabilities attending our schools and the lack of funding to fulfill the federal mandate that made their education possible. The state instituted a higher education funding formula specifically for expenses related to students with disabilities.

Work with What You Get

April 15, 1999. Student leadership is up to the voters. I applaud this, more on some days than on others.

While a majority of student leaders I have worked with have been fine leaders and scholars, there have been exceptions that tested the skills and patience of the entire staff.

In my first job in higher education, I learned from Bill Field, Dean at the University of Massachusetts, Amherst, that I had to serve all students, whether I liked them or not, whether I agreed with their beliefs or not, and whether I wanted to serve them or not. This lesson has served me well over the years and no less in the role of Vice President.

Lunch and Learn

May 24, 1999. I used to think that on becoming an SSAO I'd never have to go to student government meetings again.

Jim Rhatigan, retired Dean of Students at Wichita State University, gave me good advice when he said that whenever I was in town, I should attend the student government meeting. This I do religiously. While I give a fall and spring formal report to the undergraduate and graduate governments, I also attend to sit in the audience and listen. I learn a lot.

Following student elections and appointments, I try to meet early on with the new leaders one-on-one. Lunch is a great excuse to get to know a new student newspaper editor or senator, black student organization president, or captain of the rugby team. Whenever possible I do this in late spring or early summer so that I can form my own opinions and possibly influence their agenda for the year ahead. I freely share information, along with speculation, about what issues will be hot.

Taking a Student-Centered Position

June 17, 1999. I will honestly say that there is some danger in assuming a student-centered role.

On more than one occasion a student-friendly President has reminded me that "students don't run the institution" and "we don't always do things to please the students." Their admonition typically startles me and is never a good sign. What did I say that gave them this idea? Am I not making a reasoned and persuasive case? How did I present the situation in such a way that the facts, professional knowledge, and good judgment did not prevail?

On the other hand, I have also examined the possibility that it is a wise tactic my Presidents use to throw me off. In those instances, my response is not to retreat but simply to ask, "Why do you say that?" We immediately get back to the real topic, or we have a great dialogue about the centrality of students to our mission, decisions, and allocation of resources.

Always take the student's view. This is different from taking the student's side. Ask, "How would a student move through this policy or process?" "How does this help or hinder students in pursuing their education?" If necessary, ask these questions aloud and wait until you get a satisfactory answer.

7. Coming to Terms with the President

Where's the Boss?

August 10, 1998. I am not sure what the proper protocol is. Does one just "drop in" on this President?

A beautiful bouquet of flowers from the President greeted me on my first day on the job, but I did not see my new boss, Joe Crowley, that first week at Nevada.

After two days I decided I had better tell him I was there. To my relief, the secretarial staff greeted me warmly and told me he was out of town. On his first day back Joe came by to see me—and I was racing out to give a speech at orientation.

Getting Down to Business

August 28, 1998. My first one-on-one meeting with Joe.

In some ways, becoming a Vice President is just like any other new job. You still have to get a parking permit and learn where the bathrooms are. It was the relationship with the President that I was less sure of. How often should we meet? What did he want to hear? Did he use email? Was I to go to all the Regent meetings and write annual reports? How did I request budget items? Should I expect a performance review?

Feeling our way along, we eventually fell into a pattern that worked. I saw Joe every Monday at his cabinet meeting, and each month the two of us met to talk, more for my benefit than for his. When I needed to let him know something immediately I called. As a new Vice President, I could not have asked for a better boss. It was clearly Joe's longevity as President that created a comfortable rhythm to our work together, even in a crisis.

I was a loyal and awestruck follower. It was said that Joe Crowley could have been Governor of Nevada if he had so chosen, and I believe it. Sage, savvy politician, and wry humorist, as University President he had also been President of the NCAA, had taught many of the state's office holders, and was a doting grandfather. While working for Joe was not *the* reason I accepted the job at Nevada, it certainly was one of the top five.

Question Authority – Delicately

October 10, 1998. The President's agenda is really the institution's agenda. At least that's how I view it. Quite possibly it is the other way around, but my loyalty to my supervisor has always been fierce. Perhaps this is because I expect no less from my own staff.

I always viewed it as a major part of my job to help my supervisor achieve his or her goals, whether I worked for the Director of Residential Life, the Vice President for Student Affairs, or the President. On the one hand I relish the power they give me, but, on the other, I know that the better solution will come from a partnership.

The first six months I followed the mantra of supporting my boss in everything he wanted. After all, Joe had been President for over 20 years and my fellow Vice Presidents had been there longer than I had. On a handful of occasions I disagreed, and once or twice tried to voice it, but each time I felt I had failed and was miserable. This wasn't who I was, or wanted to be, as a professional. Was I not able to articulate a differing viewpoint? Did I lack the skills to persuade a President? Was he not listening to me?

Pushed to an extreme one day, I launched, "with all due respect," into my reasoning for an alternative course of action. The President disagreed. I restated my position with a few additional options. He countered once more. After stating what I thought was in his best interest and that of the University, I finally said, "Well, you asked for other opinions and I gave you some."

Later that day, just as I began to feel I had flopped, the President came in to my office, smiling, "Wasn't that a great meeting today?" A light went on in my head: he genuinely likes verbal sparring. It was not necessarily about disagreeing, but about offering a second opinion, another option, a new perspective. I also learned that it was nothing personal.

Challenging your supervisor is a delicate skill, best done at the right time and place, often in private. Honesty, with tact, brings you credibility and is appreciated by most strong leaders.

All in the Same Boat

January 21, 1999. Joe is under amazing pressure for this University to grow. We aren't growing, but I know we are up to the mandate.

And in fact we were. Our campus now has the highest growth rate among Nevada's institutions, but that was not the case when I arrived. The pressures to grow were all-consuming. Throughout fall semester, in a variety of cross-university meetings, people had said things like, "I'm a faculty chair and should not be spending time talking to students in an effort to recruit," or "YOU people..." should do this or do that.

I'll never forget one fairly new Dean, sitting a few seats away from the President, saying, "I've been traveling all around the state, no one knows the University, or if they do they hate us. YOU have a big problem." I could not stand it any longer. "What's this 'YOU'? How about 'WE'? WE are all in this together and have to work together to resolve it, or else WE will fail."

There was laughter, some nods, stunned looks, and I'm sure I heard a wonderful guffaw from the President. Afterwards he was ecstatic. He had appreciated my strong stance, and I felt our partnership was beginning to solidify.

Change Will Come

December 29, 2000. My President is leaving and it is sad. It's been seven months since he announced his intention to resign, and I am just now able to begin writing about it.

Life is good when the man or woman who hired you is President of your university. My first two and a half years as Vice President were even better than I anticipated. I was fully aware that Joe Crowley would retire a few years after I took the job, but I did so, knowing it was a risk.

I had never, in over 20 years in the field, worked for someone who had not hired me, and I learned that the true test of your mettle is when a new President arrives. My friend and colleague Almeda Jacks, Vice President of Student Affairs at Clemson University, says, "A change in presidents is an opportunity for new energy and new opportunities." Another colleague handed me an important lesson: "Remember that your new President is the Regents' choice. It is his vision you must now attach yourself to."

Having now been close to a presidential transition, I see just how many people are affected when there is a change at the top. No magic number of years in a job will give you security (or the hope that someone will fire you and put you out of your misery!). In my fifth year at Nevada, a vice presidential colleague was given notice to leave. He and the President had tried it for a year, and the President must have decided that was enough. Over 18 years, this colleague had run the institution and advised other campuses, the Chancellor, and even the government. In a blink he was gone. Never think, my friends, that it cannot happen to you.

While it has been different under a new President, I can validate Almeda's point that a fresh perspective has brought new energy to our campus and to my work. My loyalty to him and his great goals for the University inspires me and, as with his predecessor, it is clearly my role to help him succeed. A new President, especially one from outside the university, has a much higher need for information, advice, and honest input.

Like all good leaders, Presidents of colleges, whether new or old, need honest feedback with clear options. Let me add that a wise leader seeks a lot of advice from different people, and an even wiser leader decides which advice, if any, to follow.

8. Cultivating the Regents

Are They on My Side?

August 28, 1998. My first meeting with the Regents. I am puzzled by their lack of allegiance to the system and individual schools. Many belittle the Presidents, angrily grill those making requests, and threaten administrators.

For much of my professional life I had no contact whatsoever with Regents or trustees. As a Dean at The Evergreen State College, I had an occasional interaction with trustees, particularly concerning fee increases and presentations on student life; they were interested and very supportive.

As a new Vice President, I faced something dramatically different. First, as the Senior Student Affairs Officer, I have at least one item on every board meeting agenda. Second, Nevada's Regents oversee a state system of three community colleges, two universities, and two colleges. Their watchdog role places their allegiances with those who elected them; often, they seem to view this role as placing them against the colleges and universities.

In my first year I listened to Student Services Vice Presidents in Nevada with more seniority speak of the Regents with familiarity. They had talked to them at campus receptions or athletic events and planned or participated in community programs with Regents. These were friendships, or at least relationships, with a level of comfort and dialogue that I truly envied and wondered if I would ever have such satisfying contact.

Bonding in the Bleachers

October 17, 1998. At today's football game a Regent turns to me and says her daughter is interested in Evergreen. I ask if this is a test, since I really should be trying to talk her into sending her child to Nevada! She laughs (always a good sign) and explains many things about her daughter that make Evergreen a perfect choice.

Through good luck or through trial by fire, I have cultivated good relations with individual Regents over time. The best relationships begin as this one did. Once I find out they have teen or college-aged children, interaction flows easily around the topics of selecting a school or major, housing options, and transition issues for the whole family.

For years now, my football friend and I have had wonderful conversations about her daughter (who is doing very well at Evergreen) and about both our families. We may not always agree on matters before the board, but we work to understand each other and create mutually satisfying solutions.

Some colleagues avoid the Regents, sometimes for good reasons, but I know that this is not in the best interest of students. Over the years I have come to understand the unique demeanor of each Regent as a politician, a community leader, a supporter of public education, and as a human being. Reaching this point has varied from Regent to Regent, but it is time and effort wisely invested.

Diplomacy and Other Devices

February 16, 1999. A testy but illuminating exchange today with an audit committee member about granting refunds to students after the deadline. "You may be morally in the right, Shannon," he says, "but your staff violated Regents' policy. Instead of going on the defense and escalating the anger of some Regents, you should simply admit it and promise not to do it again."

Some hard but important lessons have come about through such feedback from Regents. That early session taught me the value of contrition. At my next appearance before the audit committee, I repeated his very words through the entire meeting as the Regents poked and prodded me. I then drafted a revision endorsed by every other campus, since they too had been violating the policy for many years, and asked the system staff to present it on behalf of all of us so that it would not be associated only with me. The Regents passed it unanimously.

Some Regents, however, seem to be in opposition no matter what, and you must resort to a political framework to secure their support. In two instances some Regents did not want to authorize bonding capacity that would allow us to build much needed residence halls to accommodate an influx of students. Logic was not persuading these Regents; clearly, other forces were coming in to play. At future board meetings, I brought parents and students from the districts of those Regents in opposition to add their voices to our appeal. By reminding the Regents of the human side of our work, and that these were the constituents who could vote them in or out, I secured unanimous support.

Tallying Things Up

June 2, 1999. I have moved from fear to great enthusiasm about going before the board. I view every agenda item as an opportunity to educate.

I try never to enter a Regents' board meeting without knowing if I have the vote. A friendly phone call or a chance conversation with a Regent at a campus event can bring me amazing insights. I never hesitate to ask for their advice. They know the voting patterns of their colleagues and often give me informed suggestions on how to approach another Regent.

Tailoring information specifically for each Regent has worked well to gain their support. Some Regents have a single important agenda that they promote with every vote. For example, one is on an admirable mission to incorporate the concerns of underrepresented populations into the work of the system and its campuses. This is very much in keeping with the mission of Student Services, and my ability to address diversity in every agenda item I present helps to forward both her cause and that of the students. Her vote is won if I can demonstrate how a policy or program enhances a multicultural student body, and lost if I cannot.

I never hesitate to ask directly for a vote of "yes" when my item comes before the board. Regardless of how I gain their support, Regents are critical partners to me as a Senior Student Affairs Officer in securing the policies, programs, and monetary adjustments necessary for my staff and I to serve students well.

9. Navigating the State System

New Fish in a Big Pond

August 12, 1998. I meet with the Vice Chancellor for Student and Academic Affairs and find her approachable, energetic, and exceptionally visionary. She has all the right books on her shelf, indicating student services knowledge, and our discussion is completely student centered.

Nevada's two universities, two colleges, and three community colleges are coordinated by a system office under the leadership of a Chancellor. Again demonstrating that it pays to be nice to everyone, the system Vice Chancellor when I arrived at the University ended up becoming Chancellor in 2000 and was highly supportive.

Over time, I sought to cultivate similar relationships with all my colleagues in the system office. The Vice Chancellors for Technology, Research, and Finance became important resources and touchstones; staff who crunched the numbers and wrote reports to the Regents proved useful allies, especially when trying to explain the unique situation at our University.

Their different perspectives often helped me to formulate a thoroughly successful plan. I listened to their warnings of political pitfalls and they offered stinging critiques when I asked. And I did ask. By staying in touch through lunches and meetings we quickly became mutual resources, and this balanced relationship gave me a chance to lead system-wide efforts to better serve Nevada students.

Some Free Legal Advice

January 15, 1999. I remember how difficult it was for our VP at Evergreen to get hold of the attorney assigned to our campus. She had to stand outside the Trustees' meeting and buttonhole him when he went to the bathroom. When we got a new woman attorney, our VP accomplished a lot more because she could actually go into the same bathroom!

I was determined not to settle for such a deal when I became a Vice President.

At Nevada, our legal counsel is in the system office and access to them is crucial. I had always been cautioned not to overuse campus counsel, in order to keep costs down, but I grew to understand that the most important reason is that you have to be prepared to follow their advice. Once you ask their advice and get an answer, it is a riskier course of action to go against their opinion than not to ask at all.

When you call the attorney, be clear in your mind about the results you want and pose your questions to that end. For example, "We want to be able to discipline disruptive students who live in private housing in the neighborhood. How can we make this happen, since it is off campus?" I once told our counsel: "We want to diversify our staff. We'd like to require that finalist pools brought to campus for interviews are diverse. How can we make that happen so it is fair and legal?"

Do not be afraid if they tell you right off that what you want is impossible. Hang in there, keep talking, face-to-face when possible, and do a little research and ask them to do some more. Maintain the attitude that you want them to help you find a way to make things happen. Legal counsel can be a strong and enduring ally.

When in Doubt, Throw a Party

March 2, 1999. As the newest Vice President in town, I've shied away from convening colleagues within the system. I finally used that as my excuse to call today's meeting, telling them I want to get to know them. Meanwhile, they all thank me for helping them to reconnect....

Whether you are a Senior Student Affairs Officer at a private or a public school, I urge you to seek out regional, state, or local colleagues for regular contact. No one knows what you are experiencing better than another Vice President for Student Services. Begin by pulling a few people together for breakfast or lunch, and expand your time together to half or whole days. A relevant agenda of problems, policies, and strategic plans makes a long drive or plane trip worthwhile.

After two years in the job I became chair of the Student Affairs Council, a coalition of Student Services Vice Presidents from each Nevada campus. (Lest you be overly impressed, I got the job because every other Vice President was interim!) It proved to be yet another example of the powerful coalitions we can create with other schools to help move our agenda along. The council's activity included design and implementation of Nevada's Millennium Scholarships, development of a funding formula for students with disabilities, and a review of regulations that put unnecessary barriers in front of today's student.

While some of my peers complained that our group did too much of the work that system officials should be doing, I found the higher profile of my chairmanship gave me a direct advantage. I was called upon frequently to report to subcommittees of the board and was commissioned to chair a task force of Academic and Student Services Vice Presidents on advising. Through this, I became better acquainted with many of the Regents and well versed on system-wide issues rather than only those pertaining to my campus.

Under the Spotlight

April 19, 1999. I go with the President to testify on the legislation to establish the Millennium Scholarships from the tobacco settlement money. The Governor shows up. We chat in the hallway – just the two of us – and I say more to the Governor in the hallway over two Styrofoam cups of coffee than I say later in the committee hearing. Nevada is an amazing state.

Another new experience as the lead Student Services administrator was my ongoing interaction with legislators. Our proximity to the capitol in Carson City surely contributed, and I often found myself there during that first spring. Our External Relations Officer, or lobbyist, portrayed my presence as a way to educate and enlighten the politicians and arranged informal information meetings with leaders of both parties where I had to answer a lot of loaded questions.

To prepare for the Millennium Scholarships debate, our University's wonderful financial aid staff gave me a crash course, so I could keep it simple but attend to every possible question the legislators might ask – which they did. The President and I co-presented to the Senate Finance Committee, the power committee, and I had been advised to give very short answers. My first was cut short by the chair after the first sentence, and I quickly learned what "short" means in politics. Anything beyond one sentence can irritate the speaker, but if he or she is on your side, you have it made.

As I came to be educated in the ways of politics, I caught on that politicians look for "something they can hang their hats on" when it comes to molding legislation. Our lobbyist would escort me to the door of the leadership chambers and leave me there to educate, enlighten, and answer questions in a way that was value-free and factually based, but never, ever lobbying for one side or the other. It was harder than it sounds, and a bit intimidating, but it was an excellent exercise in simply presenting the facts, and I came to love it.

So, This Is How It's Done

May 3, 1999. Our Governmental Relations Director regularly includes me in annual legislative dinners and ceremonies, so I can cultivate relationships with the Senate and Assembly members. He says I make his job easier; I say he is making mine more effective.

Every new Vice President benefits by forging a partnership with the governmental relations professional on campus. I frequently send ours reports and studies about students, as well as on state and national trends. He addresses the entire Student Services Division before the start of the legislative session to advise us on pending issues, and often stays for the remainder of our meeting to better inform himself about what is going on around campus.

Our strong rapport has also provided me with an entry into a world new to me, the nitty-gritty of politics. Attending formal legislative hearings is vital, sometimes simply to be seen and heard, but I learned from the veterans that Nevada's final legislation is quite literally crafted in the smoke-filled rooms of Carson City – even when it concerns directing tobacco settlement funds to students.

The more you can educate decision makers on issues, especially concerning need-based aid and assistance for nontraditional students, the easier it is to craft assistance programs. Most of those serving in public office listen, and in our state they also search for policies and programs that would make Nevada a better place for its booming population.

One such informal gathering included the state Treasurer, the Governor's staff, various legislators, a few other administrators outside the Student Affairs arena, and myself. We ate lunch and kibitzed about students, about the widows and orphans who might need or deserve the tobacco money, about why Nevada has the nation's lowest high school to college continuation rates. The opportunity to exchange views and influence those making decisions was exhilarating.

10. Surviving the Media

You Write the Script

August 20, 1998. I have my first interviews with local TV and newspapers this week. I felt I needed a crash course on everything from rates in the dining halls to the composition of our student body. Luckily, our Communications Director helped me prepare, even told me details about reporters' styles, what to look out for, what not to be put off by.

It was my good fortune to work with a pro during my first year. The Communications Director and I mentored staff who would not talk to the media and others who talked too much. She ran a series of workshops on press protocol, manner, and tips for success. The dialogue and the frequency of our media-related conversations resulted in clear channels of communication on and off campus.

Individuals who become Vice Presidents have already dealt with the media, and I have no unusual horror stories to tell. I can only say that no one can force you to say anything you do not want to say. If I don't know an answer, I ask to call them back in 15 minutes. If reporters' questions are leading me down a slippery slope, I take control of the interview to get out my message and not theirs.

I am notorious for picking out two or three points I want to make on a subject and only responding with one of those – in a clear sentence – when asked a question. This ensures that I don't say anything off the cuff, and my message is the only one they have to print or broadcast.

No Smoking Guns Allowed

January 13, 1999. Nothing – ever – is off the record.

After you have been on campus for a while, you will no doubt cultivate relationships with local reporters. This is natural; they are nice people and usually ethical. But nurture those contacts with a grain of salt. Remember that, in the end, they are just doing their job, which is to get a good story.

Sometimes our ego drives us to do silly things, and it is also in our nature to want to help a reporter get a story. Saying something is "off the record" does not guarantee that it is.

In fact, plenty of us have been burned by making that statement. We get reporters to agree not to use it in a story, and then it shows up in print the next day or on the evening news. I made that mistake once, and that was enough.

Meet the Press? Maybe Not

March 23, 1999. Some staff, campus safety in particular, believe press conferences are the way to go. I just don't see the need— it can send all the wrong messages.

I'm often told that press conferences are efficient. You handle the same questions from several reporters all at once rather than all day long. Well, let me say that fielding those questions all day, all month, or however long it takes is someone's job, but probably not yours. If not the campus police or another Vice President, then most certainly the senior information officer on campus can, should, and will do this for you when necessary.

Press conferences often appear to be publicity-seeking events, which you never want in a crisis or tragedy. It can feel like a circus and quickly turn into a feeding frenzy. One reporter sets off on a conspiracy theory or insinuates a cover-up by the university, and you are heading down a path you cannot control.

A press conference also implies that you are open to answering any question. Quite often we are not, especially after a student death or in situations involving sensitive and labor-intensive investigations. Stick to press releases that are short and sweet – just the facts. You won't speculate about things you do not know, and you won't have to deal with the unexpected in front of a room full of reporters.

Be helpful, return their calls, but don't go overboard. Most of us work in towns where the media do not stick around for long; this is just a rung on their career ladder. Get to know their successors, but remember whom you work for. A reporter does not care if you say too much, but your staff, students, and boss will. They not only care, but they may act upon your poor judgment.

11. Politics for Beginners

Embrace Your Inner Politician

September 24, 1998. Being a "politician" in the workplace is typically perceived as a terrible thing, or unprofessional; some in Student Affairs seem to assume that they can simply postpone politics until they become a Vice President.

I like to think that, in fact, being a good politician is what got us to this position. Political skill is critical to a Vice President's operational and administrative success and smooth handling of planned and unexpected change.

Never think that you are too lowly to have a voice or make an impact, and never think you are above being political. It is an honorable skill and attitude that works to your advantage on the expansive landscape that confronts a new Senior Student Affairs Officer.

In my best years I suspect I was able to navigate the politics of my University and Division because I was instinctively following some sound political rules. In my bad years, when I felt stuck and eagerly shared in mean-spirited gossip, I was doing the opposite. It did not serve my colleagues or I very well, and certainly was not in the best interest of students.

The Nature of the Beast

November 16, 1998. Larry Roper, Associate Vice Provost at Oregon State University, first clued me in to the nature of the political animal. Politics, he says, is not just about relationships, it is about managing other people's reputations.

My mom would call this being gracious, others would wrap it up with the old adage, "If you can't say anything nice, don't say anything at all." Not a day goes by that I do not manage other people's reputations. Early in my tenure, a fellow Vice President was saying one thing about my budget in public and something quite the contrary in private. My attempts to address this tension with him one-on-one were getting me nowhere. I was within an inch of bringing this up at the President's cabinet meeting to make our mutual boss aware of my concern, hoping he could help get things back on track.

But I did not. After the meeting I walked with my colleague back to his office and told him, "You know, we keep discussing this issue and the lack of resolution really frustrates me. I did not want to raise it in front of the other Vice Presidents and especially not in front of our President. I thought he might get upset. Can we work on a resolution now?"

Much to my surprise he stared me in the eyes and thanked me – thanked me! – for not raising the problem in a public setting. We sat down to talk. He applied his best listening skills and his even better problem-solving skills and gave me what I needed. I left content and he had an intact reputation.

Another important lesson is to not believe everything you hear. I had received numerous warnings, beginning during my interview, about one Vice President. People said he was two-faced, conniving, and generally not to be trusted. On my first day he was the colleague who took me out for lunch. We had an extremely useful conversation about the pressure points in enrollment growth and the state political scene. He was straightforward and offered a hand in partnership.

I rarely experienced anything other than that with him in our years working together. On occasion I had to challenge him, but applying a direct approach always produced a solution. I could be completely honest with him, and he offered help even when I did not ask. Everyone needs a colleague like this. Others' experience does not have to be your own. Keep an open mind, listen carefully, but do not automatically accept the opinions of others on the character of your colleagues.

Scare Tactics

If only I could scare my staff into keeping expenses down, increasing retention rates, and working harder!

Let me be clear. I am not an advocate of scare tactics to get things done, although to be honest, it is a tempting tool. Sheer terror can be brought about with a threatening phrase, a terse look, or – most forcefully – public humiliation. There are men and women who deliberately use all these as means to their ends.

One colleague at Nevada was feared by his staff, and I admit, I capitalized on that fact. When I wasn't getting what I needed from his staff, I merely had to mention his name and action quickly followed. What intrigues me about fear in the political arena is how others try to use it on my staff and me. Know it when you see it and deal with it immediately.

My journal is full of examples from my first year. A Regent makes an angry phone call to demand that exceptions be made to the rules. Legislators threaten cutbacks to higher education unless faculty and staff behave more accountably to the public. A reporter from the local paper uses the old technique of offering to tell "your side" of the story, lest the article look "bad for you." You can always ignore intimidation by the media.

And you can certainly choose to confront and challenge. I often ask those in positions of authority to put their request or "command" in writing so that I can file it properly. When they refuse, I ask why. Once, I asked someone to consult with the University system's attorney over whether a certain demand was permissible. I never heard back.

Politicians given to grandstanding may need to be educated. One hostile individual was making a very public attempt to destroy a policy that benefited students. Through a mutual acquaintance, I managed to get an introduction and had a conversation with her. Things calmed down for about two years. Then there was another outburst, and I simply called her to ask if it was true that she had made the statements attributed to her. We went from there, and things are quiet again. I expect I'll need to interact with her in another two years.

A Seat at the Table

March 17, 1999. Relationships are now coming about, a big leap from the initial meetings and pleasantries – this is good.

A new SSAO's political agenda is to find ways to create relations with stakeholders, influential parties, and decision makers. It is an overwhelming task: you need to identify the most important individuals and groups and prioritize your outreach efforts accordingly.

During my first few weeks I sought out and met those critical to my agenda: Vice Presidents, Academic Deans and Associate Deans, the Chair and Chair-Elect of the faculty senate, my own Division's Senate

Representatives, the Affirmative Action Officer, the Dean of the Graduate School, undergraduate and graduate Student Senate Presidents, and the City Council Member for our district and adjacent districts. As the months went on, I toured northern Nevada high schools, meeting Counselors and Principals, and later the southern rural and urban schools as well as tribal communities.

These informal meetings came to take on even greater significance after my first year. My office shares a building with the University's senior administration, and this is a tremendous advantage to staying in the loop. I began to establish a pattern of lunching with the Faculty Senate Chair every month. We've maintained this standing engagement, and it is an invaluable bridge to the academic world and academic leadership. It is one of the appointments I never break; the relationship building is too important to my work serving students.

Connections like these bring you into an inner circle, an informal but influential power grapevine. You'll get a seat at the table where you might otherwise not be invited. Advocating for the interests of Student Services is our job, and to do this you have to have access to the decision makers. Data and persuasive arguments only get you so far. It's the long-term connections, combined with collegial friendship, that often seal the deal.

Discovering What Is Already There

April 14, 1999. Many days I can easily take the other side and think through others' perceptions and opinions. But some days I cannot do this alone and need help.

One of my techniques for getting this help is to seek out the existing skills and knowledge that will allow me to think differently. This also creates political possibilities and hones my political savvy. I try to identify "complementors" – the people and organizations outside the Division or even the University with significant influence on my varied constituents. These are relationships I call upon only at pivotal moments to gain the most crucial information.

I stumbled upon one amazing ally, the State Assessment Coordinator for K-12.

Her projections on the demographics of the state's student population, combined with school board discussions on increasing graduation standards, prompted Nevada's two universities to step up a plan to raise admissions standards. Not only did her information and insights renew our confidence in our understanding of this contentious issue, but she spoke on behalf of our proposal. Given the quality of her research and the entity she represented, her 10 minutes before the Regents helped change the minds of many.

My own political style relies on working with various people in different ways. One is by building successful and innovative coalitions to deal with the most difficult issues and unexpected situations. To avoid the usual pattern of university and neighbors in a coalition against students, or university and students allied against the neighborhood, we enlisted students as members of the neighborhood advisory board. The equitable stature of all has transformed the monthly "town and gown" meetings into venues for building community around shared values.

Helping disparate and often opposing people and groups to discover what they have in common is an amazing recipe for turning possibilities into political reality. On our campus several student groups simply did not get along; they would not even communicate with one another. Students of color were galvanized in one corner of the campus, while predominantly white undergraduate leaders ran the campus from a centralized student union. Small numbers of graduate students struggled to organize, and the Greeks isolated themselves in a few off-campus houses. Animosity and rumors were rampant.

In conversations with these groups, we found that they all wanted a leadership development class. Getting representatives together for a first meeting was momentous, but first we had to clear the hurdle of defining leadership. Slowly and methodically, staff and students struggled to find one thing they had in common. They critiqued and questioned one another's ideas of leadership, shared their diverse stories of "heroes and sheroes." Things got animated, and we were off and running.

Diversity

Where is the diversity on this campus?

What I found in Reno was a small population of students of color and many different levels of awareness. "Multicultural patriots" existed in isolation on campus and their calls for passionate commitment and a plan were met with relief and joy in some quarters, but confusion, anger, and defensiveness in others.

I started with the patriots and moved ahead one person at a time to build a movement. This was not a movement in which the campus majority ruled or advice to back off and slow down was heeded. I knew it was right and nothing could stand in the way of achieving a more diverse and educated staff, as well as more students of color. It was as simple as not planning Parents' Weekend on Rosh Hashanah and as difficult as requiring diversity in the finalist pool of every search in the Division.

Let the Negotiations Begin

May 3, 1999. I'm not sure when things began to go so terribly wrong over the office space for my Division. One minute Admissions and Records was vacating a basement, and the next thing I knew every academic and finance office on campus was measuring square footage and staking out space.

I'll confess right now that I have never taken a formal counseling or student personnel class. Taught it, yes, and certainly lived it. My models and favorite theories arose over the last four or five decades, and while some SSAO roles, skills, and techniques remain tried and true, new approaches are always needed and welcome.

Our office space saga was my introduction to negotiation. Space is more precious than gold on my campus, but in my early years at Nevada there was no such thing as a space utilization committee or facilities management board. This was both good and bad. Bad in that the University's bigger concerns were not used as a guide, good because the rules of the Wild West still applied: "Possession is 9/10ths of the law."

We were moving to a brand new Student Services Building in the center of campus, no complaints there. But the run-down, depressing basement inhabited by one of our units turned out to be more valuable than I realized. I negotiated with the Vice Presidents in Academic Affairs, Finance and Administration, Development, and Diversity. In the end I split the space with Academics. Development got some of my other vacancies, Finance and Administration was just plain mad, and the Vice President for Diversity decided he was happy with the way things were, but was an important ally in the process.

My epiphany came when I realized that negotiating is not purely rational. It takes place on two levels. The first and most obvious is discussion of substance; the other level is intimate interpersonal communication. Deborah Kolb and Judith Williams call this "Shadow Negotiation" in their book of the same name. As we bargained over this decrepit basement, we were also negotiating how we were going to negotiate. After I had heartily inserted myself into the fray, I made it clear that meeting the interests and needs of students would command our attention and guide our negotiations.

Once I established this expectation, the eventual winners aligned with me and the students through some strategically brilliant twists and turns. We began to coalesce as an alliance, with a sense of our own space, and those on the periphery of this conversation went away – some disgruntled, others understanding. Trust me, I did plenty of compromising, conceding, and thinking creatively, all of which led me to discover the important skill of connecting in a negotiation process.

Finding One's Voice

July 22, 1999. Being pushy is not my style. But in the fine art of negotiating, and in politics, people make demands, and so must I.

I came to look at it not as being pushy but rather as finding my voice. One disadvantage of being new is that you may not yet have crafted your agenda to the point where you can easily sell it. But as you gather survey data, present needs analyses, and share national models, your preparedness makes you strong. Your self-confidence grows and you're better able to hold your own. Don't worry about making everyone happy: the price of keeping the peace can be too high for your division.

There's a little strategy I call "tit for tat." If another division approaches me with a proposal – "You give us this, and we'll give you that" – I don't accept it right away. If I do, they'll ask for more. I try to slow the process down, tell them I'll think about it, and put forth my own demands.

Four times in my first year the Vice President for Finance and Administration asked me to fold Police Services into my Division. The first time I just laughed, but by the third time I reminded him that the unit had once been in Student Services and the staff still remembered how it had consumed 80% of their time to the detriment of everything else.

The fourth and final time the Vice President told me that he had cleaned up the unit and it was ready for me to take over. I asked what he wanted in return. When he said "nothing," I knew I definitely did not want it. For the life of me I couldn't think of anything I wanted from him. I looked him in the eye and told him never to offer me Police Services again. That's finding one's voice.

12. Thinking Strategically

Some Things Are Sacred

September 5, 1998. I have not come to change things nor was I hired to incite change. But it's happening regardless and causing pockets of chaos, stagnation, innovation, and exhaustion!

The Student Services strategic plan that I inherited at Nevada had a little more than two years left to go. Reading it prior to my interview, I found it emphasized the undergraduate experience and its major strength was that it was written in conjunction with the Academic Master Plan. What it seemed to lack, aside from attention to graduate students, was a passionate vision that would lead the University to an exciting place and serve the needs of the state.

I was chomping at the bit to begin a new one, but I would never have dared to do so. I believe strategic plans to be sacred. Yes, they must be flexible, tweaked now and again, but a plan's greatest value is that it sets clear priorities toward which all resources are devoted. To change those dramatically is to undermine the research, thinking, and strategizing that went on before. So I waited...and waited...and waited.

But this does not mean I did nothing.

The Vision Thing

October 10, 1998. Every day, inevitably, I get the same question: "What is YOUR vision?"

And my answer? Usually something between the cautious retort – "Your vision is my vision" – that new people often give (and I'll admit I was tempted), and the Power Point presentation with a 10-point plan for the Division. I had some sense of where we should go, I genuinely believed people wanted to hear it, and, to be honest, I certainly wanted to tell it.

Many of us think strategic planning is not important, or just a simple routine; you set goals that will take five years to accomplish and you are done. If that's how you think of strategic planning, then you are missing the excitement it brings, the innovation it commands, and the sizzle it puts back into a campus. Most of all, it sets you and your division on the path to becoming a vital and strategic contributor to the institution.

My definition of strategic planning is drawn from my own experience and a number of authors, including Olsen and Eadie, Bryson and Steiner. It is a disciplined effort to produce fundamental decisions and actions that shape and guide an organization. Exemplary outcomes of great strategic planning are the result of effective information gathering, brutally honest self-assessment, fearless exploration of all the alternatives, and an emphasis on precedents as well as the implications of present decisions.

Strategic planning is "opportunity seeking" – you craft the relationship between Student Services and the rest of the University environment. It is the process of determining what an organization intends to be in the future, finding the best future with and for your division. Strategic planning facilitates communication within all levels and across units within the division to ignite broader participation among all those interested. It also:

- Minimizes the element of surprise and maximizes the ability to effectively manage change
- Helps all parts of an organization work together to achieve organizational goals
- Provides a common source of information
- Manages, rather than reacts to, change
- Measures performance against established standards

But the central objective in strategic planning is to position Student Services so that it can shape and exploit its environment, and to do this you have to fully understand that environment and how it is changing.

Think Strategically, Act Creatively

November 15, 1998. I emphasize again and again that it is strategic thinking and acting that are important, not strategic planning.

Student Services Divisions and the institutions in which they reside are dynamic environments. Even without a plan, thinking and acting strategically are crucial to our success and some would say survivability. In her book *Strategic Thinking and the New Science*, Sanders defines strategic planning as having insight about the present and foresight about the future.

When you think strategically about something it requires you to commit resources, to prioritize clearly, and to follow through on key decisions. I used to think this took courage. It does not. It takes an almost unwavering commitment and discipline, so as not to stray down a more colorful path or get lured into different initiatives by offers of money or other resources.

Strategic acts are highly imaginative, but creative thinking does not just happen. Collaboration is one of creativity's best-kept secrets. Thirteen people worked with Michelangelo on the Sistine Chapel; Walt Disney's wife Lillian convinced him not to name the mouse Mortimer but Mickey. In my experience creativity is nurtured by learning, so be sure to create a process that allows for questions, beginning with "What is most important to Student Services?" through "Who will be our students?" and "What role will learning play?" and ending with "How will we pay for it?"

Know Thy Budget – I

December 2, 1998. When I try to elicit the staff's thoughts on our Division's goals and vision, I usually get awkward silence, a little whining, and then always the theme that there is not enough money.

No money? This was the best-budgeted Division I had ever been a part of and certainly the healthiest University. These people did not know the true meaning of "no money" and I told them so. They were astonished, sure that I was wrong. That meeting ended in a truce, but it's been an ongoing battle and one that I am slowly winning.

How?

First of all, I realized that most people did not know their own budgets. There were lots of myths floating around about which offices got all the money and which were suffering as a result. I learned that there was no accounting whatsoever in big-ticket categories like phone and postage expenses. All anyone focused on was a stagnant operating budget. Yet at the end of the first year I found that we had a $60,000 surplus. This was embarrassing: how did that happen, where was the money? Why, in the very departments complaining that they did not have any money!

This, more than anything, helped me to educate the staff on their budget capacity. I also monitor the budget much more closely to avoid a surplus by moving funds to the traditionally depleted areas in early spring. The beauty of strategic planning is that it helps us spend the money we have in ways agreed upon by us all.

We reach these agreements, or priorities, outside the budget process in a realm I call the "void." Think and act strategically before you have to make budget decisions. Forget about staffing, dollars, regulations, and timelines. Attaching money to the plan hinders the ability to dream, create a vision, and think creatively.

Remind yourself and every staff member that whining provides no solutions. It has long been forbidden in our Division. Emotional hand wringing may be an honest response, but it is the hard data from user surveys, learning outcomes, and needs assessment that help me defend an idea or initiative when sitting at the budget table.

This became my most powerful tool in combating the fatalistic attitude that nothing would change, everything would get worse, and we were victims of the Legislature, Regents, Governor, or, most typically, the Administration.

Walking the Walk

December 15, 1998. I used to think organizational values were silly things that served no useful purpose in our work. Yet again, I was wrong. I inherited a strategic plan that states no values, but this gives us an opportunity to ask and answer the question: "What do we all believe?"

Values align people. The process of arriving at and then organizing work around values strengthens commitment to working for common goals. One of our Division's most useful conversations my first year was identifying the gaps between what we say we believe and how we actually perform. Everybody took part in this, including students – we all had to change habits, practices, and attitudes.

Here are a few examples from our staff self-evaluations:

- "We say we value a diverse student body, but I have been unwilling to keep our office open past five to help students taking night classes."
- "If pursuit of knowledge is truly a value, then I need to sign up for a class and start working on a degree."
- "Quality is usually not what I'm thinking when spending our budget. I'm just so used to doing more with less."
- "How do I make a difference in students' lives if all I do is input data? I suppose if I put the data in incorrectly I'll make a terrible difference."

Call it corny, but we all got so enthusiastic about our values that we printed them on our Division T-shirts and stationery: "Pursuit of Knowledge, Diversity, Quality, Safe Environment, and Vision." These common values create our unity. Better still, our essential and enduring tenets do not require external justification. Whoever said, "The most important thing in life is to decide what is most important" is right. Once we did that, we went at it hammer and tongs, laughing, risking, and struggling all the way.

Add and Subtract

February 9, 1999. The original strategic plan is still intact, but we are revising, adding, and letting some parts fall naturally by the wayside. If anyone screams, I'll know we've hit a nerve and take it as a signal to revisit.

No one screamed. To be honest, I was not sure most even acknowledged the plan in their daily work lives and annual goals. While this naturally occurs with a strategic plan in its waning years, it did make it easier for me to work with my Student Services colleagues to set a course of action leading up to the next strategic planning process.

Identifying strategic issues is at the heart of the strategic planning process. The term "add-on" suggests something trivial, but ours were quite the opposite. Critical add-ons brought attention to graduate students, with a specific emphasis on affordable housing and financial assistance.

Even more important was the broader issue of diversity. I was not hearing it discussed or seeing it implemented in any significant way. This campus still planned Parent's Weekend on Rosh Hashanah; there was no office catering specifically to the needs of GLBT students, nor were these students seeking such assistance; our own staff was not diverse. Even the absence of the tension that one normally finds in a dynamically diverse environment told me we were missing the mark and had a lot of important work to do. Another add-on was technology. Like many campuses, our online services and professional competencies were in their infancy. Some of our counselors refused to use their computers; for a technology inventory in each office they listed copy machine and paper shredder! We eventually inventoried staff technological knowledge and capabilities to arrange instruction for much-needed skill acquisition.

We also focused on both growth and retention. An odd combination, but the pressure to increase enrollment had created a culture where recruitment was the main focus. Enrollment received an inordinate amount of attention, which made everyone else in Student Services engaged in the important work of retention feel like second-class citizens.

We did not ignore growth, but instead of talking about numbers, we began to define who should make up those numbers. In 60 seconds we "generated" the list: low-income, first generation students from southern Nevada, adult reentry students, students of color, students with families, students who have no idea what they want to major in. This got people excited, and I got a glimpse of our values in action.

As we followed the plan to its completion, I began to sprinkle more messages about our Division's values and mission into meetings, speeches, and one-on-one discussions. There was conflict, of course, but more often than not it drew people together rather than tore them apart. We were, after all, deconstructing that which was familiar, and venturing out to build something – we were not yet sure what – new. Our companions any given week ranged from anxiety and fear to exhilaration and optimism.

Know Thy Budget – II

April 6, 1999. How a Vice President handles the budget is closely observed and will be remembered forever.

There is a great story about a college where late one Sunday night the phone rang in every Vice President's home. It was the President and he wanted them in his office immediately. A fire? Student death? Scandalous reasons for a resignation? They all hurriedly dressed and raced to the quiet campus. No one knew what this was about, although they knew their President could be a bit quirky.

The President's office was eerily dim. Peering in, the VPs spotted piles of papers on the conference table. They opened the door to find their boss dressed from head to toe in surgical garb, mask over his mouth, and medical instruments in each hand, exclaiming, "We're going to perform surgery on this budget!"

True or not, this story indicates how a budget takes center stage in every institution and in the lives of every Vice President, especially a new one for Student Services. When it comes to budgets, much is the same at all higher education institutions, but they vary in rhythm, tone, and protocol. Deciphering budget subtleties accurately can ensure fiscal success, and failure to do so can mean doom.

There are, however, scores of all too true stories, from many campuses including my own, of misspent funds and lost allocations due to Vice Presidents' mistaken trust in others. Stay on your guard. When it comes to money, people will do shady, inappropriate, and even unethical things. Knowing every thing there is to know about your budget is the surest way to avoid such occurrences.

By the time we become a Vice President for Student Services we should have a lot of experience building, monitoring, and cutting a budget. Some VPs have a staff member responsible for budgets, but many, like me, do not. Regardless, you should know your budget backwards and forwards. Trust only yourself to know where the money is coming from and where it is going. Read the paperwork before you sign it and never worry that you appear ignorant. Ask a lot of questions during your first month, first year, and every year thereafter.

My Division tackles the budget on a monthly basis in regular staff meetings of all three Assistant Vice Presidents, and we also discuss it weekly in the spring. We inform ourselves in a collaborative process that fosters greater accountability, tests the mettle of the staff, and gives evidence of my trust in their judgment.

And Cut Thy Budget

April 30, 1999. Some staff believe that anticipating reductions is a bad idea, that it demonstrates that we can "take a hit" and still do our work. To me, the long-term political ramifications of not contributing to the solution would be much worse – Student Services is already renowned for spending money and not producing revenue.

Many might argue with me on this, but I believe firmly that a Vice President for Student Services should avoid asking for special status and protection from cuts whenever possible. My own experience is that in order to be seen as an equal player, you have to participate in both the good and bad times. The political capital will return to benefit you, your division, and its programs and services tenfold.

But how do you decide where to make the cuts? Sometimes across the board is appropriate, but not as often as selective reductions, which are more in keeping with strategic thinking, planning, and outcomes. An inspiring exercise is to pretend that you are starting over. Write down the total sum of your division budget that is not restricted and ask your staff to build an exemplary Student Services Division within this budget. Small interdivisional groups of staff return amazing ideas that become templates for the immediate and long-term future.

A common strategy is to take 5% back from every unit in the division at the very beginning of the new fiscal year; this gives a new Vice

President some funds to accomplish some "quick wins." I was reluctant to do this my first two years. These were lean times and I also felt it undermined empowering people to create and implement their dreams. I did, however, implement this strategy in my third year. At the start of my fifth year, the Governor asked for a 5% budget cut; as we had earmarked it for the next phase of our strategic plan, we had the requested amount ready to deliver.

A self-imposed hiring freeze can allow you to slow down and think. Don't be in a hurry to fill every vacancy. You and your staff should discuss the "what ifs," including what if you never fill this job. Explore how the job description might be changed, if it can be accomplished just as well by a graduate student, or whether the salary could be better spent on another position. Look for duplication. We found the women's center, counseling center, and sexual assault prevention program were duplicating some educational efforts, and we redirected talented personnel to important retention programs.

Having come from a school where travel was severely limited, I found quite a bit going on in Nevada. While not restricting it outright, I did ask Directors and Assistant Vice Presidents to review the cost and purposes of travel in their division. Merely looking at the long lists resulted in immediate changes. We requested that staff present, rather than just attend, professional conferences, which had a spin-off as people developed new skills and gave exposure to the great ideas being implemented on our campus.

Mandatory fees are always controversial but increasingly necessary, and students are becoming more willing to pay for services and programs that they find of value. Search your division for services where no or low fees are charged. I found that to be the case in our career services, tutoring, and national university exchange programs. It might seem like "nickel and diming," but the totals do add up. It also allowed us to send up a trial balloon: no student walked away from a valuable service and most paid for it without fuss. The programs that students did not value quickly fell by the wayside.

We also found that the student fee-based program board and student government fiscal allocation committee were interested in contributing to worthwhile services. Student allocations to the free campus safety escort service kept the highly utilized program alive. When a campus-wide cut in student wages left the free tutoring services in jeopardy, it was students who told us to go ahead and charge. They provided us with a small amount of money for students who demonstrated fiscal hardship.

High Noon in June

June 6, 1999. I leave the student government retreat early to work on my budget presentation to the cabinet tomorrow. I'm glad we decided not to give up the chance for new initiatives despite having to reduce elsewhere. It is a forced reallocation process....Now the politicking begins!

As I prepared to move to Nevada, the interim Vice President, Dave Hansen, called regularly to advise me of budget developments for the upcoming fiscal year, beginning July 1. New issues arose on a daily basis – opportunities, setbacks, co-funding initiatives, attempts to retract promised dollars – it was like a TV mini-series. During one conversation near the end of June, I told Dave, "I've already learned one important lesson: Don't be away from campus in June." He laughed, "That's for sure!"

June 1999 was, not surprisingly, full of budget maneuvering. In our first presidential cabinet meeting about budget decisions, the President peered at me over the top of his glasses and said, "This isn't budget work or accounting going on here – it's all politics." Another lesson duly noted.

In the week prior to my budget presentation I asked every other Vice President to stop by to chat about budget needs. I came to see common threads and began to form coalitions for securing certain enhancements. One successful strategy to secure funds was to partner fiscally with other divisions. We obtained a higher priority and some much-needed funding by partnering our safety escort service with a request for additional campus police from Administration and Finance.

The Waiting Ends

June 20, 1999. Yet again, a staff member says to me in a meeting, "Just tell us what to do." I cannot bring myself to do that, but as a leader I sometimes feel adrift without a strategic plan to call our own.

Despite occasional frustrations, I still believe it was in everyone's best interest for me to spend my first year seeking to understand the context and culture of our Division, its departments, and role in the University.

I stuck to my belief that the success of our strategic plan would lie in the process we developed. Later that year, a small task group of Student Services staff developed the process we would follow in 2000. The strategic planning group was chaired by a Financial Aid Counselor, chosen because she had a reputation for being a levelheaded, hard-working, and quiet leader. Her committee consisted of an Assistant Vice President, the receptionist in the housing office, a handful of Student Services Directors, and several graduate and undergraduate students, some leaders and some not.

I gave them four guiding principles and then left them on their own. These were:

1. Assessment would be an ongoing activity and integrated into decisions.
2. Everyone would be invited to participate, and communication would be frequent and in various forms.
3. People outside Student Services needed to be heard.
4. The plan needed to be ready for implementation by January 2001.

It was as though I was a sponsor to the process. My ability to stand aside, listen, cheerlead, and clear barriers became the definition of leadership needed. My title and authority would sometimes come into play, when my opinion was sought I would give it.

The fact that a committee of Student Services staff developed the process attracted champions of our strategic plan. Their collective leadership provided dialogue, discussion, and creativity and resulted in a highly successful plan. Implementation is as important as writing a good plan, if not more so, and I found that it was after the exciting first year that my personal leadership was more vital.

We pulled together the strategic planning groups from 1999 and 2000 to help us develop an implementation plan and presented it to Directors and then to the entire Division for feedback. We also established strategic implementation teams for the different priorities, each chaired by an individual with a particular talent, skill, and investment in the outcome. Their work on the teams is not a side activity but part of their regular jobs. Online updates and Division-wide meetings keep information flowing, and presentations on accomplishments are now a ritual at the annual Student Services retreat.

Living in the Future

August 21, 1999. With all the change going on in the world, why would we want to leave the future of Student Services to chance or tradition?

Looking back on the development of our strategic plan, one clear result is that we became futurists. First, we gathered the data, predictions, and trends on a national, regional, and local basis. Second, and more importantly, we were futurists in terms of articulating the future we wanted to create for ourselves, our campus colleagues, and our current and future students.

Questions and answers helped us gain better self-understanding and chart our own course. Thinking, acting, and planning strategically foster organizational buy-in as each staff member develops a relationship with the realities of tradition, circumstances, and demographics. It also engages everyone in decisions related to budgeting outside of the budget process.

It is hard to argue with the plan. Reallocation, elimination, and the occasional budget enhancement are all outlined without a mention of money. Priorities are followed until the funds run out. Strategic items that are not a priority or have been identified as weaknesses are put on hold or gradually eliminated. Disassociating money from strategic thinking is the most fiscally responsible method of executing a budget available to a Vice President.

Let me stress that strategic planning is not a cure-all. It is, however, an extremely beneficial way to accomplish a number of important objectives, especially as a new Vice President. It was probably fortunate that I could not begin the process right away. The time I spent listening, reading, observing, questioning, and learning during that first year was time well spent, as was working hard to gain the trust of others in and outside the Division.

Having said that, some of you will need to develop a strategic plan immediately upon becoming a Vice President – and how lucky for you! The process will ensure a great leadership experience for both you and your staff. You will quickly learn about the strengths and weaknesses of your team and the goals and visions held by your staff and students. Acting with this knowledge, you are bound to lead an influential movement that creates a lively learning environment for your community.

13. Epilogue

Learning is Leading

June 13, 1999. I am attending the NASPA Regional SSAO Retreat, Franciscan Renewal Center, Portland, Oregon. Exactly one year ago I sat in this same room attending this retreat as a soon-to-be SSAO. I was finishing my work at Evergreen and preparing for my first vice presidency. I have come full circle. What a year. There are so many things I still must learn. Am I assertive enough? Political enough? What will it take to become an exemplary Vice President?

Education, institutes, years of experience with increasing responsibility, strong mentors, an excellent staff, extensive reading, and on-the-job lessons contribute to the development of a great Senior Student Affairs Officer. This book is – excuse the cliché – one of the lessons learned.

The story will surely be different for each and every new Vice President of Student Affairs. There is no single correct way, or reason, to do this job. Some colleagues never sought nor expected to become a Vice President. Others have held the dream in their heads for decades. Some have no educational background in college student development or higher education administration, while others are steeped in the field and its research. People bring masters' in business and doctorates in sociology to the task and meet with much success – and probably a few whispers from the purists on staff.

What seems to matter most is that they want to do it with all their head and heart. There is nothing worse than a reluctant leader. If you accept the leadership role, then be a leader. Be someone who makes your staff and students proud as you establish partnerships, advocate effectively, and promote the student-centered agenda on your campus. What impresses me most in new Vice Presidents is their understanding that they cannot know or do it all. Their sincere interest and deepest commitment is to make their college or university the best possible place for students to learn and grow, and become amazing scholars and citizens long beyond commencement day.

Bennis and Townsend write that "the journey of discovery has everything to do with reflecting upon your experience. That's why we recommend to executives they keep journals." I pass on my journey, with its successes and failures, to others. Wisdom and guidance are, after all, part of our educational culture. While this book is based largely on my own experience as a first-time Senior Student Affairs

Officer, I realize that my actions and opinions have been largely shaped by mentors in my career and life. So in some ways this is their advice too.

Plenty of people will disagree with the advice I give. That's fine. Let them write their own books. But one of the joys of this profession is the willingness of colleagues to share successes and failures, advice and insights, freely and willingly. As I say to my students, this is my advice: Take it or leave it, but at least I can sleep well tonight knowing I shared it with you.

References

References

Bankston, J. (2002). *Robert Jarvik and the first artificial heart*. Bear, DE: Mitchell Lane.

Bennis, W., and Townsend, R. (1997). *Reinventing leadership: Strategies that empower the organization*. New York: Morrow.

Bolman, L., and Deal, T. (1997). *Reframing organizations: Artistry, choice and leadership*. San Francisco: Jossey-Bass.

Bryson, J. (1995). *Strategic planning and nonprofit organizations*. San Francisco: Jossey- Bass.

Christensen, C., Aaron, S., and Clark, W. (2002). *The internet and the university: Forum 2001* (from *Educause Review*, 2003, *38*(1) 44-54).

Collins, J. (2001, January 1). Level five leadership. *Harvard Business Review*, 79.

Eadie, D.C., and Steinbacher, R. (1985). Strategic agenda management: A marriage of organizational development and strategic planning. *Public Administration Review, 45,* 424-430.

Howe, N. (1992). *Generations: The history of America's future, 1584 to 2069*. New York: Morrow.

Kolb, D., and Williams, J. (2000). *The shadow negotiation*. New York: Simon and Schuster.

MacKenzie, G. (1998). *Orbiting the giant hairball: A corporate fool's guide to surviving with grace*. New York: Penguin Putnam.

Olsen, J.B., and Eadie, D.C. (1982). *The game plan: Governance with foresight*. Washington, DC: Council of State Planning Agencies.

Sample, S. (2002). *The contrarian's guide to leadership*. New York: Wiley.

Sanders, I. T. (1998). *Strategic thinking and the new science*. New York: The Free Press.

Smith, C. (1997). *Merlin factor: Keys to the corporate kingdom*. Hampshire, England: Ashgate.

Steiner, G.A., Miner, J.B., and Gray, E.R. (1982). *Management policy and strategy* (2d edition). Old Tappan, NJ: Macmillan.

The Wingspread Group on Higher Education (1993). *An American imperative: Higher expectations for higher education*. Racine, WI: The Johnson Foundation.

Index